Firestone Books
Success Begins Here

An Inspector Calls Revision Guide for GCSE

This guide is also dyslexia-friendly!

Marcus Dalrymple

Series Editor: Nicola Walsh

Firestone Books' no-nonsense guides have all you need to do brilliantly at your English Literature GCSE

firestonebooks.com

An Inspector Calls: Revision Guide for GCSE
Dyslexia-Friendly Edition
Marcus Dalrymple

This dyslexia-friendly edition has a large easy-to-read font, minimal italics and capital letters, large line spacing, and is printed on cream paper – all combining to ensure an easier reading experience.

Series Editor: Nicola Walsh

Text © Marcus Dalrymple
Revision and Exam Help © Nicola Walsh

Cover © XL Book Cover Design
xlbookcoverdesign.co.uk

2021 Edition

ISBN-13: 9781909608436

Published by Firestone Books

firestonebooks.com

~ CONTENTS ~

Background information

The play – summary and analysis

Characters

Themes

Form, structure and language

Key quotations and glossary

Revision and exam help

Our fabulous new revision guides are out now!

Revision Guides for GCSE

- Dr Jekyll and Mr Hyde
- A Christmas Carol
- Macbeth
- English Language

25 Key Quotations for GCSE

- Romeo and Juliet
- A Christmas Carol
- Macbeth
- Dr Jekyll and Mr Hyde
- An Inspector Calls

But that's not all! We've also got a host of annotation-friendly editions, containing oodles of space for you to fill with those all-important notes:

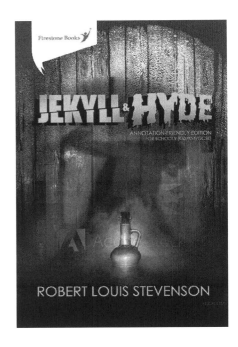

Annotation-Friendly Editions

- Dr Jekyll and Mr Hyde
- An Inspector Calls
- A Christmas Carol
- Romeo and Juliet
- Macbeth

… and lots more!

And we've got **all** these books available in super-helpful **dyslexia-friendly** and **large print** editions too!

Available through Amazon, Waterstones, and all good bookshops!

Quick tip: when you see an asterisk after a word, it means you can find the word or phrase in the glossary on page 92 of this book.

~ Background information ~

Priestley's life

John Boynton Priestley was born on 13 September 1894 in Bradford, Yorkshire where he was brought up in a middle-class home. His father was a teacher. Priestley's grandparents were mill workers and his childhood home was a place where socialist* ideas were often discussed. In Rain upon Godshill (1939) he wrote of his visits to 'grandparents and uncles and aunts who still lived in the wretched little back-to-back houses in the long, dark streets behind the mills,' which gave him experience of real working-class life and people. These early influences come across in many of his plays including An Inspector Calls, in which he exposes exploitation* and oppression*, particularly of the poor. In the play we see this in the Birlings' treatment of Eva Smith and other workers who were fired for striking.

During the First World War Priestley fought on the Western Front in Belgium. He was gassed and injured when a trench collapsed on him and was sent home. He never forgot his experiences of war and the horrors he had witnessed. In 1919, he was given an educational grant by the government and studied Political Science and Modern History at Trinity Hall, Cambridge. On leaving university, Priestley worked as a proofreader and freelance writer for the publishing company, Bodley Head. His articles for the Times Literary Supplement established his reputation as a writer.

J.B. Priestley wrote seven works of travel writing and an autobiography in addition to seven volumes of social history and over twenty novels of which The Good Companions (1929) was his first big success. During the thirties and forties, he concentrated on writing plays. He wrote forty plays in all, many of which expressed his socialist beliefs. In particular, he wrote about the inequalities between the classes in Britain.

During the Second World War, Priestley managed to write books and to broadcast a radio programme called Postscripts every weekend. These bulletins were very influential and expressed his faith in the ordinary people of Britain. Many of the views he expressed in Postscripts are also raised in An Inspector Calls. For example, he called for greater social responsibility from all classes in society in much the same way as the Inspector does in the play.

J.B. Priestley was very interested in politics, but he was not a member of any political party. In 1944, he stood as an independent candidate for Parliament and although he was unsuccessful, he remained a patriotic* socialist. In 1945 he visited the Soviet Union where An Inspector Calls had its first performance. His form of socialism was based on compassion for his fellow man – the kind of compassion and caring that the Inspector wishes to draw out of those he questions in An Inspector Calls. J.B. Priestley was one of the most popular and prolific* authors of his day and was awarded the Order of Merit in 1977. He died in 1984.

Priestley's Britain

Despite Mr Birling's confidence about the future, the reality was that Britain from 1912 onwards was turbulent. The First World War began in 1914, followed by a time of industrial unrest. In 1926 there was a

General Strike*, caused by cuts in miners' wages and there was mass unemployment during the Depression*. This was a time of economic crisis which began with the Wall Street* stock market crash in 1929 leading to loss of jobs and poverty worldwide. Furthermore, the rise of Nazism in Hitler's Germany brought international unrest and fear throughout the thirties.

The British government at the time was seen to be doing very little about these problems. During the Second World War (which began in 1939) many people became convinced that when the war ended, they had to try to create a new, fairer world in peacetime. J.B. Priestley's wartime broadcasts expressed this strongly and so does An Inspector Calls.

An Inspector Calls can therefore be seen as a 'time play'. An example of this is the straightforward use of hindsight. Hindsight is the understanding of an event or situation only after it has happened. Early in Act One when Mr Birling gives his account of how things can only get better, he is spectacularly wrong:

- **He claims that the Titanic is unsinkable:** 'The Titanic… every luxury, unsinkable...' – the ship didn't complete its maiden voyage.

- **He predicts that war with Germany will not happen:** 'You will hear some people say that war is inevitable. And to that I say fiddlesticks!' – it started two years later.

- **He says there will be no problems with labour relations:** 'You'll be living in a world that'll forgotten all these Capital versus Labour agitations,' – the General Strike took place in 1926.

- **In 1940 there will be peace,** 'Let's say in 1940…..There will be peace and prosperity and rapid progress' – Britain was under constant air attack by German bombers.

The audience at the end of the war would have appreciated his dramatic irony (when the audience watching a play understands what is going on in a situation while the characters are unaware of what is happening). Everything Birling claimed would not happen, happened. This reveals how blinkered and blind Birling is to society and events occurring around him.

Setting

The setting of An Inspector Calls is important in several ways. Priestley sets the play in the industrial city of Brumley. This is not a real place but one that he created, perhaps using his memories of his own childhood in Bradford or perhaps based on the Midland city of Birmingham. Brumley is typical of many towns where the factory owners like Arthur Birling, who provided much-needed jobs, were able to run things as they wanted without fear of being challenged. Although it is a fictional place, Priestley provides the audience with a lot of information about it:

- The town, for example, has a Lord Mayor and a police force with its own Chief Constable, suggesting that it is a place of some importance. Furthermore, there has been a recent visit by a member of the Royal Family and Arthur Birling clearly feels that being Lord Mayor and his work in local politics will have made him enough of a public figure locally to justify his being given a knighthood.

- The existence of the Brumley Women's Charity Organization, with which Mrs Birling is involved, indicates that there are many poor women in the town in need of help. Such organisations, which relied upon the financial support of rich people, were frequently found in large industrial towns and cities during the Victorian* and

Edwardian* periods. It was these same rich supporters who decided who should receive help and who should not.

By setting the play before the First World War, Priestley could make the most of the social divisions of the day. As well as the wrongs done by the Birling family, we are also told of the behaviour of Alderman Meggarty (described as a drunk and a womaniser). This suggests that J.B. Priestley was making a point that the family were not the only ones whose actions had a destructive effect on others. We therefore get a picture of a time when the underprivileged (people like Eva Smith) and the powerless (such as poor workers demanding higher wages) are the victims of rich and powerful families such as the Birlings and Crofts.

Capitalism and socialism

The term capitalism* is summed up by Mr Birling's attitude that a man should only look after himself and his family. It is an economic and political system in which a country's trade and industry are controlled by private owners, such as Arthur Birling, for profit.

Socialism* is the political and economic theory that is the opposite of capitalism. It is based on giving the workers (the people who make and manufacture goods) the profit from their work directly rather than the proceeds of their work being taken by factory bosses like Birling. Eva Smith (a worker) is mistreated by her capitalist boss (Arthur Birling). In his final speech, the Inspector warns that it is only through socialism ('one body') that mankind can hope to prevent such tragedies in the future.

Class

Social position and class were far more important in 1912 than they are today. Following the dramatic expansion of industry throughout the 19th century, many men who had invested in coal, iron and steel, pottery and textiles had made large fortunes. Men like Arthur Birling may have come from a relatively poor background, but their new wealth allowed them to climb up the social ladder. Marriage between these newly rich families and the upper-class (people like Lady Croft) helped to secure new social positions.

Many of these businessmen like Sir George Croft, were knighted for their work with industry and this too helped to improve their social standing. Although wealth did allow some people to move from a lower to a higher class, generally in Edwardian times there was a great divide between social classes and little opportunity to move between them.

Workers' rights

The rights of workers like Eva Smith were not taken seriously by many employers. Birling was all too typical of the greedy employers of that time. Life might have been good for him, but it was not good for his workers. The working-classes had to work hard for very little money often in factories owned by the middle-classes such as The Crofts and Birlings. The Labour Party, founded by James Keir Hardie in 1893, campaigned for the rights of workers and for better wages and encouraged strikes to protest and demand better working conditions. Unfortunately, the party did not gather enough support until the twenties and did not have much impact in influencing powerful factory owners to provide better working conditions for their workers.

Priestley's purpose

In 1945, when An Inspector Calls was written and first performed, Priestley is warning of the consequences of not making the social changes that were necessary. He had fought in the First World War and was one of the soldiers who had been promised that they would return to a 'fit country for heroes to live in.' Instead, he and countless others had returned home in 1918 to the terrible reality of unemployment, strikes and protests. The Welfare State was a new programme introduced by the Labour Government in 1942 to protect the health and well-being of its citizens, especially the lower classes, by means of grants, pensions, and other benefits. This included the establishment of the National Health Service (NHS) and free education for all.

The play can therefore be understood in two different contexts. It is an example of a post-war drama, exploring the economic, social and political issues exposed by the Second World War and its immediate aftermath, such as socialism versus capitalism. But An Inspector Calls is also an historical play, set at a very precise time in Edwardian England shortly before the First World War. This creates moments of dramatic irony throughout the play that are clearly understood by post-war audiences. The false façade* of respectability presented by the Birling family at the beginning of the play, Eva Smith's tragic death and the cracks in the Birling family that the Inspector exposes, foreshadow the devastating social, political and economic consequences of the two world wars that Priestley witnessed.

As the play progresses, the Inspector's point is put across more and more forcefully. Each character's involvement with Eva Smith adds to the Inspector's argument and he becomes not only a spokesman for the working-class but a voice for the conscience which the Birlings and Gerald seem to lack. The characters, especially the older ones, are increasingly shown to be hypocrites*. The Inspector points out what would happen if injustice and inequality continue: 'If men will not learn the lesson, then they will be taught it in fire and blood and anguish.' His moral tone reaches its peak when Priestley's political message is expressed in the Inspector's final speech: 'We do not live alone. We are members of one body', he says before departing.

The play is a challenge to the audience to think about how many more disasters might lie ahead if we don't learn from past mistakes. This message is as relevant now as it was in 1945.

Progress and revision check

1. What parts of the setting could be based on real towns in 1912?

2. What are the major differences between capitalism and socialism?

3. Who represents capitalism in the play?

4. Who represents socialism?

5. Which characters represent the upper-class in the play?

6. Which character most represents the working-class?

7. What kind of problems did soldiers returning from World War One encounter?

8. In what ways is the play about the years before World War One and after World War Two?

9. What was Priestley's purpose for writing the play?

10. What schemes were introduced by the Labour Party in 1942?

~ The play – summary and analysis ~

Who's who

The Inspector

Inspector Goole (ghoul), as his name suggests, is a mysterious character who turns up at the Birlings' home to make enquiries about a local girl Eva Smith, who he claims has died recently. He seems to know a lot about the Birlings. However, at the end of the play, it's revealed he wasn't really a police inspector.

Arthur Birling

Arthur Birling is the owner of Birling & Co. He is a wealthy factory owner. He is married to Sybil Birling and they have two children: Sheila and Eric.

Sybil Birling

Sybil, married to Arthur and mother of Eric and Sheila, is a cold woman. She is the chairwoman of a local women's charity.

Sheila

Sheila is the eldest of the two Birling children and at the beginning of the play is engaged to Gerald Croft. She increasingly becomes the family's social conscience and is the character that changes the most during the play.

Eric

Eric is the youngest of the Birling children and a university graduate. It is suggested throughout the play that he has a drinking problem. Like Sheila, he regrets his actions and is prepared to change his behaviour.

Gerald Croft

Gerald Croft is engaged to Sheila Birling. He is the son of Sir George and Lady Croft who are Birling's business rivals. He has been invited to dinner to celebrate the engagement. Gerald had an affair with Daisy Renton.

Eva Smith/Daisy Renton

Although we never see Eva Smith, she is a presence in the play and it is around her death and the events that led to her suicide that the drama focuses. She was employed at Birling & Co. and later at Milwards shop in Brumley.

Edna

Edna is the Birlings' cook and maid.

The Play

Act one

The play begins just after Arthur Birling and his wife Sybil have held a family dinner party to celebrate the engagement of Sheila Birling and Gerald Croft. Their grown-up son Eric is also present. Mr Birling is pleased with the match because of the closer business ties which he hopes the marriage will bring.

In a celebratory mood, Mr Birling shares his views on industry and makes speeches about his hopes for the future and how he expects Sheila and Gerald to live in a world without conflict or war. When the ladies and Eric have left the room, he goes on to tell Gerald that a man only needs to care for himself and his family and that they should ignore the 'cranks' who claim that everybody has a responsibility to care for everybody else in society. The evening is interrupted by the arrival of Inspector Goole, who is making enquiries about the suicide of a young woman.

Mr Birling admits he had employed Eva Smith in his factory two years ago after the Inspector shows him a photograph of the young woman, but he goes on to tell the Inspector that he had fired her for being one of the leaders of a strike for higher wages. Gerald Croft believes that Arthur Birling did the right thing and supports what he did. However, both Sheila and Eric feel that their father had been too hard on the young woman. When Sheila asks to see the photograph, she confesses that she had the same girl fired from her job as a shop assistant at Milwards simply because the girl had looked much prettier in a dress than she did.

The Inspector appears to have mysterious, prior knowledge of the family's dealing with Eva Smith. When he announces that Eva Smith had changed her name to Daisy Renton, it is clear from Gerald's reaction that he also knew her. By the end of the Act the Inspector has begun to infer that the entire family, along with others in the community, share a joint responsibility for the misery which prompted Eva Smith to commit suicide. The Act ends with Sheila warning Gerald not to try to hide anything from the Inspector.

Analysis

An introduction to the Birlings

The house, as well as the 'decanter* of port, cigar box and cigarettes' demonstrate the comfortable lifestyle of the middle-class Birling family. The stage direction 'heavily comfortable but not cosy,' suggests that although the Birling household is materially well-off, it is not happy or united. This is an important first indication into the Birlings' life. All is not as it seems.

We are introduced to the characters for the first time at the beginning of Act One. Gerald appears confident and well-mannered. Mrs Birling comes across as cold, whilst Mr Birling is in a good mood but cannot resist lecturing the younger generation about his opinions: 'The Titanic…every luxury…unsinkable.' His comments show how wrong he can be: the Titanic would sink on its maiden voyage; there would be two World Wars; social unrest, unemployment and strikes would mark the next three decades. It is particularly significant that the Inspector's arrival happens just as Birling is demonstrating so much self-importance. This is ironic because the Inspector is there to try to teach them all about real social responsibility. The Birlings' family life is held together by secrets and polite behaviour which the Inspector is about to disrupt. Sheila is described as lively in contrast to Eric who is presented as being awkward and almost drunk. When Sheila accuses her brother of being 'squiffy' – tipsy - it warns us that his parents do not know about his drinking habits. There are clearly things about Sheila and Eric that their parents are unaware of.

Mr Birling is keen to explain that the port is the same as the one bought by Gerald's father. 'Finchley told me it's exactly the same port your father gets from him.' Birling sees Sir George Croft as his social superior and his comment about the port demonstrates that he is a social climber and wishes to be seen as an equal to Sir George. Birling sees a knighthood as an appropriate reward for his involvement in local politics as well as a way for him to become an equal of Sir George Croft. His speeches, however, show he has no intention of contributing anything of real value to the community: 'We employers are coming together to see that our interests, the interests of capital are properly protected'. The repeated use of 'we' and 'our' demonstrates that he is only interested in himself and yet he is still happy to accept the city's reward in the form of a knighthood.

There are hints of conflict beneath the surface. There are clearly differences between what is expected of men and women. Men are supposed to be busy with 'work' and the world of 'public affairs.' Women are supposed to be interested in family, 'shopping' and social etiquette*. A significant moment is when Gerald produces an engagement ring for Sheila. The ring is the one Gerald wishes Sheila to have and not one which she has chosen, which hints to his dominant status in their relationship. The play has many subtle touches such as this to show

how men and women were treated differently and had different roles. Another example of this is when the women leave the men to talk about business and worldly matters, subjects which it was presumed women had no interest in or knowledge of. In Edwardian times, it was considered acceptable for a man to have an affair, particularly if it was with a woman of a lower class. It was certainly not acceptable for middle- class women to have lovers.

Birling's interrogation

To begin with, Birling and Gerald are not worried by the Inspector's visit. They regard the police as their servants and protectors. Birling's manner towards the Inspector changes from being relaxed and rude to aggressive as he finds himself having to defend his actions: 'I was alderman for years – and mayor two years ago…I know the Brumley police officers pretty well.' He believes that he is superior to a mere policeman and that his importance in local politics can influence the Inspector. Shortly afterwards, however, when the Inspector begins his interrogation, his tone changes: '(somewhat impatiently) look there is nothing mysterious or scandalous about this business…' This is why, later on, Mr and Mrs Birling object to the way the Inspector speaks to them.

Birling has no sense of loyalty or duty as their boss towards his workers and refuses to consider their need for more money if it means he must have less profit. Birling's use of the word 'duty' is also revealing. A duty is normally an obligation. This tells us something about Birling's lack of feeling and empathy for others and about how little he values people. He feels he has no responsibility to anyone but his family.

Birling admits that Eva Smith had good qualities; she was a good worker, but he disliked her willingness to voice her opinions. Gerald's support of Birling shows that he too cares more for profits than for the treatment of his workers. Even though Sheila is told several times to leave the room by her parents, she insists that it is her 'duty' to stay and listen to the whole story and to learn who was responsible for the young woman's death. Sheila feels a genuine, moral* sense of 'duty,' where Birling does not.

There is a marked contrast between how the Inspector speaks and how Mr and Mrs Birling talk. The Inspector speaks bluntly and to the point. He says the girl 'burnt her insides out.' This graphic manner of talking contrasts with the polite way the Birlings and Gerald address each other. To the Birlings, manners are more important than the truth.

Sheila's interrogation

With the Inspector out of the room, Sheila takes on his role as interrogator in her questioning of Gerald. As the play progresses, Sheila increasingly becomes the family's conscience.

Sheila's initial distress at having her happy evening spoiled is juxtaposed* by the greater unhappiness of the dead girl's life. This is shown when the Inspector says, 'a nasty mess somebody's made of it', revealing that he is not concerned about breaking up the happy party but would rather get to the truth.

The Inspector suggests that Sheila misused her social status as Birling's daughter to blackmail the shop into firing Eva Smith: 'I'd persuade mother to close our account with them.' He shows her how spoilt her actions have been, 'because I was in a furious temper', and their devastating consequences. Sheila's regret seems genuine: 'If I could help her now, I would.' She has learnt a lesson and she is determined never to act so unfairly again.

By the end of the first Act, it becomes clear that Mr and Mrs Birling and Gerald are less emotional than both Eric and Sheila. They also show less remorse about the consequences of their actions. Priestley is perhaps suggesting that the younger generation will have more of a sense of social responsibility than the older, Edwardian generation. The Act closes with the Inspector once again opening the door and entering the room, just as Sheila is telling Gerald that the Inspector has a mysterious knowledge of the family's dealings with Eva Smith. 'Of course he knows,' she says to Gerald, just before 'the door opens slowly and the Inspector appears.' This is significant as it re-emphasises the control that the Inspector has and reminds the audience of his first appearance at the end of the dinner.

Despite Birling's and others' attempts to show that Eva Smith was merely a victim of circumstance, Priestley clearly intends the audience to feel that much of her suffering could have been avoided and that she had been treated harshly both at the factory and at Milwards.

Act two

The tension between Sheila and Gerald from the previous Act is still noticeable. Gerald confesses that the previous year, during the spring, he met Daisy Renton and she had become his mistress. He claims he had ended the affair six months later. Sheila is visibly angry and hurt by Gerald's admission, but she feels a certain respect for the honesty of his confession.

Believing she is superior to the Inspector, Mrs Birling attempts to intimidate him and tries to control events. This leads her to treat him with less respect than the other characters have done. She continues to remind the Inspector (and the audience) of her respected position in the community, but Sheila has already realised that outward respectability is no guarantee of good moral behaviour. Meanwhile, Mr Birling is becoming increasingly concerned about the possibility of a public scandal. He is mainly worried about the effect it could have on his chances of receiving a knighthood.

Sheila feels that it is pointless to try to block the Inspector's enquiries and she is proved to be right. She is concerned that her mother will also be blamed for Eva Smith's suffering and tries to warn her against attempting to hide things from the Inspector. Whilst Eric is out of the room, Mrs Birling is forced to admit that Eva Smith had come to her for help two weeks earlier but had been refused. It emerges that she was pregnant, and suspicion now falls on Eric as being the father of the unborn child.

Analysis

Sheila's reaction

We are shown the hypocrisy* of Gerald's attempts to shield Sheila from hearing the unpleasant details of Eva Smith's life and death since Eva herself had not been spared what was unpleasant and disturbing for her: 'I think Miss Birling should be excused any more of this questioning...It's bound to be unpleasant...' Gerald says to the Inspector, to which the Inspector replies, 'well we know one young woman who wasn't (protected) against...disturbing things.' Here, Priestley, through the Inspector, is attempting to demonstrate that Eva and Sheila are both equal and therefore if Eva has experienced unpleasantness, there is no reason for Sheila to be shielded from it.

The Inspector appears to understand Sheila's feelings in a strange mysterious way: 'Miss Birling has just been made to understand what she did to this girl…' He does not spare her feelings, however, and we see Sheila's sense of guilt because of his blunt manner of describing the circumstances of Eva Smith's death: 'But she died in misery and agony – hating life.' Sheila is struck by the truth of what the Inspector says even though she cannot properly understand his power at this time: 'That's true you know. I don't understand about you,' she says staring at him.

The Inspector already senses that both Sheila and Eric are more easily touched by the tragedy of Eva Smith's death. Someone like Mrs Birling, however, who believes her social status puts her above being concerned for Eva Smith, is less moved: 'You seem to have made a great impression on this child Inspector,' to which the Inspector replies, 'we often do on the young ones, they're more impressionable.' This hints that the younger Birlings are more open to the Inspector's interrogation and perhaps more willing to change. Here, Priestley is suggesting that it is the younger generation that are society's hope for the future and the ones who need to change for the better.

Sheila is once again impressed by the Inspector's ability to make people confess. She is more aware of the family's responsibility for what has happened and is deeply affected by Eva Smith's story. Sheila's tone with Gerald has changed since the revelations of his affair. She becomes increasingly sarcastic with him: 'Well we didn't think you meant Buckingham Palace,' she says to him when referring to the Palace Bar.

Her sarcastic tone is a significant contrast to the way she spoke to him earlier in the play, which suggests that she has learned her lesson and this experience has changed her from the innocent girl she once was, to a more mature, socially-aware woman.

Sheila seems to be the only character who understands the Inspector's ability to draw out the family's dark secrets. When she summarises what has happened to Eva Smith, it reminds us of the greed, jealousy and selfishness they have all demonstrated. Mr and Mrs Birling continue to try to intimidate the Inspector by using their social status and remind him of his relatively humble social position. The Inspector remains unimpressed. He emphasises the ideas of duty and responsibility; qualities which the family have yet to show.

Gerald and Mrs Birling's interrogation

Even though the audience are more likely to blame Gerald for what happens to Daisy Renton, we can appreciate his reasons for rescuing her from Alderman Meggarty. Gerald's honest confession helps to add to our knowledge of when things happened to Eva Smith. It also makes him a more sympathetic character. Priestley makes Daisy Renton seem vulnerable by comparing her prettiness and youth to the 'hard dough-faced women.'

The timing of events leading to Eva's death is brought almost up to date when it is revealed that Mrs Birling saw her just two weeks before, but there remains a gap between the end of Gerald's affair with Eva Smith and Mrs Birling's meeting with her. Mrs Birling has a strong opinion of how people of different classes should behave. Her prejudice and dislike of Eva's manner echo Mr Birling's views when he said, 'She had a lot to say – far too much so she had to go.' It also reminds us of Sheila's anger when she had said Eva Smith had been very 'impertinent.' Each character had used their power and position to harm her.

Mrs Birling is not influenced or affected by anything Sheila says and only at the end of the Act does she begin to acknowledge that she may have made a mistake. Her belief that the father 'should be made an example of,' only serves to set a trap for her and Eric.

When we learn that Eva Smith has used the name Mrs Birling, on approaching the charity for financial help, and goes on to describe the father of her unborn child, we are shown clues as to what might happen next. It is significant too, that Eric is the only one who has not yet been questioned, as he is the last to have seen Eva alive. Priestley effectively leaves the Act on a cliffhanger to reflect the Birlings' ignorance about Eric's involvement.

Act three

Eric confesses to having had a relationship with Daisy Renton and also to be the father of her unborn child. Moreover, he admits to stealing money from his father's firm to try to support her. He is horrified to learn that his mother had refused to help Eva and he blames her for Eva's death and the death of the unborn child. What family unity there had been before the Inspector's arrival, begins to fall apart. The Inspector has completed his investigations and has shown that each of them had a part in ruining Eva's life. He makes a dramatic speech about the consequences of irresponsible behaviour before promptly leaving.

Between them, Gerald and Mr Birling are gradually able to prove that the man was not a real police inspector. This raises doubts as to whether they have all been talking about the same girl and about whether any girl had killed herself. On ringing the hospital, they are told that there is no record of any girl dying there that afternoon. There is a general feeling of relief at hearing this information although Sheila and Eric still feel guilty for their actions and they seem to have been changed for the better by what has happened. At this point the phone rings. Mr Birling answers it to find that it is the police calling. He is told that a young woman has just died on her way to the hospital and an inspector is on his way to make enquiries about her death.

Analysis

Eric's interrogation

Eric's guilt begins to be made clear. Our earlier suspicions about Eric are confirmed and there are unpleasant revelations about his relationship with Eva Smith. Mrs Birling's self-confidence begins to crack, and Eric's confession starts to make it crumble. The Inspector now has complete control of the events. This is shown in the way he overrules Mr Birling and allows Eric to have a drink: 'I know he's your son and this is your house - but look at him!'

It is revealed that both Eric and Gerald had met Eva Smith at the Palace Theatre Bar and both thought she was different from the prostitutes usually found there. It is significant that both men meet Eva Smith there; Priestley is once again suggesting that the men of the higher classes are happy to use and abuse lower-class women without giving them a second thought. Eric's meeting with Eva in November, two months after Gerald's affair had ended, conveniently fills in the gap in Eva Smith's history. Eric is careful in how he describes what he did, so he simply says, 'that's what happened.' This lack of information prepares the audience for the horror of the reality of what happened.

Eric's admissions are vague; he does not even mention her name. This uncertainty about her identity is convenient later in the play when her very existence is questioned by Gerald and Mr Birling. Furthermore, Eric had told Eva his name. As he was the father of her child, it was natural for her to use his name when applying to the Brumley Women's Charity Organisation for help. His language in the all-male gathering is blunter than when the ladies are present.

Mr Birling is concerned there might be a possible scandal when Eric reveals he stole company funds. Once again, his first thoughts are to protect himself and his family's good name, not the plight of the poor woman.

The Inspector exposes the family and Gerald's weaknesses when he reminds each of them of what they did to the Eva Smith. This shows that his task is almost complete, and it leaves them to think back on their part in Eva's death and builds up the sense of guilt before the Inspector's final speech.

His final speech focuses on responsibility. His reference to what will happen in the future makes him sound like a Biblical prophet* and suggests he is something more than an ordinary police inspector. The speech is also used to deliver Priestley's own strong social message. If attitudes towards the lower classes do not change, society will be doomed.

As the Inspector leaves, there is a noticeable change of mood. Everyone present is clearly shaken and their feeling of self-satisfaction has been destroyed.

Generational conflict

Mr Birling feels that Eric is the only one who has behaved in a way which might be seen as directly causing Eva's death. Eric however stresses that the responsibility is shared equally by all of them. His point refers us back to the Inspector's 'chain of events.'

Sheila has faced the truth about herself better than her parents and Gerald have done. She is shocked and disappointed that there has been no real change in their attitudes. Like Eric, she thinks it is irrelevant whether or not the Inspector was a real policeman. For her, the important thing is that his visit should make them think about and accept their responsibilities towards the rest of society.

Birling believes they were all rash in making their confessions. He can excuse his own admissions since he feels he fired Eva Smith for acceptable reasons. He reverts to the ideas that he expressed to Gerald and Eric in Act One, dismissing anyone who expresses sympathy, feelings or concerns for others as dangerous and unstable.

It is Gerald who first casts doubt on the identity of the Inspector. He uses the uncertainty about Eva Smith's name and the fact that no one else saw the photograph to suggest that there might have been several girls: one girl that Mr Birling fired, another that Sheila had dismissed from Milwards, a third girl that he had an affair with and yet another that Eric had met and who probably tried to get help from Mrs Birling. The irony here is that if they had treated four different girls badly, it would have been far worse, but the family fail to consider this.

Arthur and Sybil join Gerald in trying to improve their own tattered reputations by discrediting the Inspector. In believing that they have been tricked, they feel that they have been cleared of their irresponsible behaviour.

Eric and Sheila do not share the relief felt by the others. They have been so deeply affected by the evening's events that the truth of the Inspector's identity makes no difference to them. They cannot forget what they have done.

Progress and revision check

1. What do the stage directions about the house suggest about the Birling family?

2. What event are the Birlings celebrating at the start of the play?

3. How are the two younger Birlings presented at the beginning of the play?

4. What is ironic about the various statements Birling makes about the future?

5. In what way does Birling demonstrate a lack of loyalty towards his workers?

6. How is Gerald hypocritical in wanting to shield Sheila from unpleasant revelations?

7. Why do you think the younger Birlings are more open to the Inspector?

8. How does the photograph of the girl and the diary help the Inspector?

9. Why is Eric's vague admission that he had met Eva, convenient?

10. Why is it significant that both Eric and Gerald meet Daisy at the Palace Bar?

~ The play – summary and analysis ~

~ Characters ~

The Inspector

The word 'inspector' suggests someone who looks closely at things and this is his role in the events of the play. The name 'Goole' is the name of a seaport town on the River Humber and perhaps suggests that the Inspector is 'fishing for information.' The name also sounds like 'ghoul'– someone with an interest in death; a spirit which is said to take fresh life from corpses. It is arguable that the Inspector's existence is a result of Eva Smith's death or perhaps he is a spirit sent on her behalf to torment the characters? Priestley didn't want to promote a single interpretation of who the Inspector really is. His dramatic power lies in the mysterious character and it keeps the tension rising until the end of the play.

The Inspector is described as creating 'an impression of massiveness, solidity and purposefulness,' and he seems to grow in size with each new, fresh revelation. As the other characters gradually break down under his questioning, he remains solid. He arrives just as Mr Birling is stating that every man should look out for himself and his family. The Inspector's role is to show the family that this is not the case. Throughout the play he consistently points out that people's behaviour and attitudes affect others in the community. He stresses that everyone has a social responsibility towards others. This is summed up in his final, dramatic speech.

It is the Inspector, with his 'fishing' that exposes all the family's secrets. From the moment of his arrival he seems different to the other characters. He is serious, and the sad news he brings contrasts with the happy celebrations that have been going on, which reflects his intention to break down the ignorance that the higher classes demonstrate towards the lower classes.

The Inspector's control

Despite the social status of Birling and Gerald, the Inspector is not intimidated by them and it is he, not them, that controls the conversation and the progress of the investigation. He even seems to control what people say. Sheila tells Gerald, 'somehow he makes you.' Those characters who resist telling the Inspector the truth suffer more than those who are open. He says to Gerald, 'If you are easy with me, I'm easy with you.' However, he begins to lose patience with Birling: 'Don't stammer and yammer at me again man!' The exclamation mark is evidence of his impatience with their nonsense. Mrs Birling resists telling the truth the most and the Inspector is accordingly the harshest with her: 'I think you did something terribly wrong.'

The Inspector's use of Eva Smith's diary and letter helps him build up a picture of the pain and suffering that the young woman endured, and he uses this to put pressure on the family. The Inspector is therefore both an outsider, seeking information and an insider who already knows everything about Gerald and the Birlings and their dealings with Eva Smith.

The Inspector as Priestley's mouthpiece

The Inspector could be seen as personifying Priestley's views on how people should behave towards others. He is the play's social conscience. He warns the family, 'You see we have to share something. If there is nothing else, we have to share our guilt,' suggesting that all people should share everything including their wealth and if not that, then guilt for society's past wrongs. He points out that social responsibilities become greater as wealth and privileges increase. If people make more money, they have a greater responsibility to financially help those less fortunate.

He is also the voice of compassion in the play, not only towards Eva Smith but characters like Sheila, who show remorse for their actions. Unlike a real policeman, he is more concerned with right and wrong than what is lawful or unlawful. This is significant as the Birlings and Gerald technically committed no crimes and therefore do not deserve investigation from the police. He is not inspecting them with the law, but with morals instead. Where the Birlings value manners and politeness, the Inspector is more concerned with truth and justice.

The Inspector's function

Inspector Goole has several functions in the play:

- He acts as the storyteller linking the separate incidents into one storyline.

- He often supplies dates or fills in the background.

- He behaves like a priest to each character, encouraging them to confess their sins for what happened to Eva Smith. Significantly he neither judges nor punishes the characters but allows them to judge themselves and learn from their mistakes.

- He plays the traditional role of a policeman in a 'whodunnit' story, slowly uncovering the truth through careful questioning and piecing together evidence with clever insight. Unlike a 'whodunnit' however, no one is charged or arrested for any crime.

Inspector Goole sheds light on all the concerns that Priestley had at the time of writing the play around age, gender, class and social responsibility. Priestley uses the Inspector to make the audience question their own behaviour and morality and hopes that they will learn some lessons, as some of the Birlings do. However, the failure of the older generation to learn from their mistakes means that an inspector must return at the end of the play. Priestley has brought the audience full circle and once again we find Birling interrupted mid-sentence with a phone call in which he is informed that a policeman is on his way 'to ask some questions.' Priestley is suggesting that moral inspection will continue until all have learned their lesson. The issues the Inspector highlights are just as relevant to a modern-day audience as they were in 1946.

Finally, is the Inspector's investigation successful? There is the possibility that Eric and Sheila may have learned enough to change their ways but the others, even at the end, strongly resist any change. Post-war audiences would have appreciated the Inspector's prediction of a lesson that 'will be taught …in fire and blood and anguish,' unless people change, because both he and the audience witnessed the horrors of the Second World War and its catastrophic effects on society.

Mr Birling

Stage directions are in many ways a direct insight into the playwright's* intentions regarding the play, and Priestley's opening directions are no exception in helping the audience to learn about Mr Birling. The Birlings' home, like Arthur Birling is 'substantial' and 'heavily comfortable.' He is described as 'heavy looking' and 'portentous*.' The set, therefore is clearly symbolic. It is the house of a 'prosperous manufacturer' but it is not 'cosy and homelike.' These directions say as much about Birling as they do about his house. Like his home, Birling is heavily built with a domineering personality. Moreover, he is a wealthy factory owner, but although his home has the trappings of wealth, it is not a warm, affectionate place, which foreshadows Birling's lack of care towards those less fortunate than himself.

Birling as a social climber and bully

Throughout the opening of Act One, Birling is linked to indulgence through the clearing away of the dessert plates and the champagne glasses and the replacing of them with cigars and port. He is self-confident, but his upbringing makes him less socially aware and polite than either his wife or Gerald Croft. He sees the engagement of Gerald and Sheila as being good for business and he and his wife believe that public office is a way of moving into the upper-middle class. He is so obsessed about such things that he even feels a little uneasy about Gerald marrying his daughter, sensing that Gerald's parents may feel that their son is marrying, 'beneath himself.' Birling is at great pains to tell Gerald that 'it's exactly the same port your father gets,' in the hope of impressing his prospective son-in-law, although his sense of self-importance is slightly punctured by Sheila's observation that 'you don't know all about port, do you?'

For Birling, the marriage between Gerald and his daughter has more to do with his ability to secure his place in society rather than with Sheila's future happiness. Like his wife, he doesn't really care about his children's emotional needs but is more concerned about how the rest of society view him.

His view of his own self-importance leads him to:

- Try to use his social status to frighten the Inspector.
- Control, bully and stamp his authority on Eric and Sheila.
- Be concerned about the effect of a scandal on his chances of a knighthood.

Mr Birling is a successful businessman and factory owner who has been active in local politics and has had the honour of being Lord Mayor. However, he is blind both to the consequences of his own actions and to events in the larger world. He makes predictions about the future – the unsinkability of the Titanic; the impossibility of war; and the promise of technology – which would have been believed by many in 1912 but would have been laughed at by audiences in 1945. Mr Birling can see no reason why nations should go to war and upset the businessman's quest for profit. It never occurs to him that people might value other things more highly. He is in many ways a caricature* of the businessmen of his time.

It is central to the play that his attitude that, 'a man has to mind his own business and look after his own,' is shown to be wrong by the confessions that the Inspector draws out. He sees himself as an upholder of all the right values and as a guardian of proper behaviour but is exposed as self-centred and heartless. He begins by trying to put the Inspector in his place by emphasising his position in society. Birling does not change his views or attitudes over the course of the play. Although he despises weakness in others and shows his anger at the foolish behaviour of Eric and Sheila, he cannot see that his actions towards Eva Smith were wrong and we feel that if events were repeated, he would still fire her. He feels this was and still is the right attitude for a man of business. He sees nothing strange in wanting to protect Sheila from the unpleasantness of Eva's life and death, yet feels no guilt at not having protected Eva Smith.

When the play was written after World War Two in 1945, there was no form of welfare from the government to help the poor. Mr Birling represents greedy businessmen who only care about themselves. Priestley uses him to show the audience that the Eva Smiths of the world will continue to suffer if people like Birling remain in positions of power.

Birling's lack of responsibility

Arthur Birling is clearly not a good parent. He shows little understanding of his family and believes his daughter and wife achieve self-respect through clothing and talk of shopping, weddings and social etiquette. Like his wife, he fails to see that his son has a drink problem and blames his son for being 'spoilt' without realising that he is the father who spoilt him. As Mrs Birling lets slip, her husband is a man who 'has important work to do' and therefore must spend 'all his time and energy on his business.' His factory clearly takes priority over his family.

Arthur Birling, like his wife, has learnt nothing from the evening's experience. Before the Inspector's departure he insists he would 'give thousands' in order to change what had happened and then immediately blames Eric for the situation before predicting 'a public scandal' and asking, 'who here will suffer from that more than I will?' He claims, towards the end of Act Three, to have 'learnt plenty tonight' but then attempts to brush his actions under the carpet and blames the family for falling for the Inspector's trickery.

He contradicts himself and we see that his regret is not real when the Inspector has gone, he suggests that, 'the whole thing is different now' and congratulates himself on having avoided a scandal. He cannot understand Sheila and Eric's insistence that there is something to be learnt. He has only ever been concerned about his public image rather than his social responsibility.

Through Birling, Priestley lets us see someone who is blindly wrong about people and events and blinkered to his own failings. Perhaps he is suggesting that as long as their public reputation is safe, people like Birling will never change.

Mrs Birling

For most audiences, Mrs Birling is perhaps the least sympathetic character in the play. She is described as a 'rather cold woman and her husband's social superior' and she is very conscious of social position, especially her own. She seems more concerned about maintaining polite, upper-class behaviour than her social responsibility, shown for example in the way she scolds her husband for his comment about the quality of the meal: 'Arthur you're not supposed to say such things'. Comments like this make her seem out of touch with what really matters and it is this coldness that make audiences unsympathetic towards her.

At the start of the play, Mrs Birling is sitting opposite her husband at the table, which was both a convention of middle-class families at the time and also a sign of the emotional distance between them. Furthermore, the reference to Mrs Birling being her husband's 'superior' is significant. During the time the play was set (and written) the rising middle-classes – men like Mr Birling – were seeking to marry more established women from the upper-classes. In exchange for status and social acceptance, they brought financial wealth and security. For Mrs Birling we get the sense that the match with her husband was less than ideal: 'When you are married,' she tells Sheila, 'you'll realise that men with important work to do sometimes have to spend nearly all their time and energy on their business.' For Sheila, this is a clear message that not only will she need to 'realise' this, she will also have to 'simply get used to it.' This suggests that just as Eric is turning into Birling, Sheila too will become like her mother – cold and distant, marrying for convenience rather than for love.

Mrs Birling as a neglectful mother and irresponsible citizen

Despite the audience being given the impression that the family is close at the very start of the play, it becomes quickly apparent that Mrs Birling does not really know her children: 'The things you girls pick up these days,' she exclaims to Sheila when her daughter uses the word 'squiffy.' She also reacts with shock when she finds out about Eric's drinking in Act Two. She is 'staggered' and insists 'it isn't true' since he's 'only a boy.' To Mrs Birling, her daughter and son are still both 'children.' Sheila is a 'girl' not a woman who is engaged to be married, a girl who needs to be told to 'go to bed' and be protected from unpleasantness, whilst Eric is a 'boy' not a man. In effect, Mrs Birling is an absent mother - not physically, but emotionally detached and this is perhaps best reflected in the fact that she is absent from the stage for much of Act One and Act Two.

Is Mrs Birling genuinely unaware of what is going on around her or is she deliberately blind to anything she does not wish to see? Consider how she dismisses the news of Eva Smith's suicide: she cannot see how the death of a 'lower-class' person could be of any interest to the Birlings. When she is criticised, Mrs Birling hides behind words like 'respectable,' 'duty' and 'deserving.' She thinks that people from lower classes have different feelings from her own. Eva Smith's request for financial help was 'giving herself ridiculous airs' and 'claiming elaborate fine feelings.' Her snobbishness is further emphasised when the Inspector leaves and she criticises the others for not standing firm against someone who is their social inferior as she had done. 'He certainly didn't make me confess,' she says adamantly. She seems to take pride in her reaction to the Inspector, when ironically her reaction is perhaps the most despicable to the audience.

Furthermore, Mrs Birling likes to be perceived as being respectable through her work with The Brumley Women's Charity Organisation, which she claims has done 'a great deal of useful work helping deserving cases.' The charity, like her family, is another area which she seeks to control. She is a 'prominent' member and able to use her influence to refuse help to the likes of Eva Smith, whilst claiming to have done 'my duty.' Her lack of understanding of how other people live is shown in her snobbish comments about 'a girl of that sort' and in her unwillingness to believe Eva Smith's reasons for refusing to take the stolen money or marry the foolish young man responsible for her pregnancy. Like her husband, she claims to have higher, more noble standards and beliefs than she actually does.

She remains untouched by the Inspector's questioning and refuses to see how her actions could have been responsible for Eva Smith's death. We can clearly see how her refusal to help her could easily have been what finally led to Eva Smith's suicide, yet it is only when she realises that Eric was the child's father and so her actions resulted in the death of her own grandchild, that she begins to show any signs of weakening.

The speed with which she recovers when the Inspector's leaves emphasises how cold and unsympathetic a character she is.

Mrs Birling's hypocrisy

Priestley reveals Mrs Birling to be a hypocrite in several ways:

- She claims to be shocked by Eric's drinking, 'you're not that type, you don't get drunk,' and the talk of improper relationships with Eva Smith, yet she is determined to hear Eric's confession: 'I simply couldn't stay in there (referring to the drawing room). I had to know what is happening.'

- She is quite content to blame the father of the child. When it became clear that the young man is her son, she is not prepared to own up to her previous comments until Sheila brings them up again.

- Earlier on, she condemned Gerald's 'disgusting affair' but seems quite willing to forget about it once the Inspector has gone and everything seems to return to 'normal.'

- The relief that she demonstrates when Gerald suggests he wasn't a real inspector reflects her desire to remain untouched by outside events and to maintain the appearance of respectability.

Like her husband, Mrs Birling ends the play having failed to learn from her mistakes and wanting to go back to how things were. She is an example, Priestley suggests, of certain people who will never change and why the play ends as it began.

Sheila Birling

Sheila is described as a 'very pretty girl in her early twenties, very pleased with life and rather excited.' Early in the play she is playful and rather self-centred, enjoying the attention that her engagement is bringing her. Furthermore, she appears to be a little immature and easily led. Her behaviour is childish, and she does what her parents tell her: 'I'm sorry Daddy actually I was listening.' Here Sheila shows her lack of maturity in the way she reacts to her father. She is quick to apologise, she is keen to behave well, and she also refers to her father as 'Daddy', a childish term. At the start of the play, Sheila seems materialistic, apparently caring more about the engagement ring than the actual engagement with her comment, 'now I really feel engaged.' This says a lot about her relationship to Gerald, namely that it is based on wealth and status rather than on love. She seems shallow too by her reaction to the Inspector's revelation about Eva Smith: she wishes that he 'hadn't told her' because she had 'been so happy tonight' and all she seems interested in is what Eva Smith looked like: 'What was she like? Quite young? Pretty?' The Sheila we first meet at the beginning of the play soon disappears when she gains the knowledge of what has happened.

Sheila's transformation

Sheila's curiosity when she finds her father, Eric and Gerald with the Inspector is at first superficial; she merely wishes to know who he is and why he has come. However, she soon shows a sensitive side to her nature and is moved by the news of Eva Smith's death. Unlike her father, she responds to Eva Smith as a person not cheap labour. 'But these girls aren't cheap labour – they're people,' she says to her father. Moreover, she is prepared to criticise her father: 'I think that was a mean thing to do,' which shows that although she is spoilt and selfish, she has the potential to change.

When Sheila realises that her own jealousy and bad temper had led to Eva Smith losing her job at the shop, she is sorry. Yet we also see her sorrow is linked to her feeling of regret that she will not be able to go back to a favourite shop and so her streak of selfishness is still there. It should be noted that her jealous complaint against Eva Smith is probably the worst action of all, based merely on her own arrogance – she thought Eva Smith looked prettier in the dress than she did. By the end of Act One, Sheila is already aware of the influence of the Inspector and is beginning to question how deep his knowledge goes. She warns Gerald 'Of course he knows. And I hate to think how much he knows that we don't know yet.'

Sheila grows stronger and more sympathetic as the play goes on. As the play progresses, Sheila's character develops, and she begins to stand up for herself: 'I tell you - whoever that inspector was, it was anything but a joke.' The change in Sheila here is clear. She has become more confident, using phrases such as 'I tell you'. The events of the evening have made her aware of the serious impact her actions can have.

She is obviously upset by Gerald's confession but is strong enough to cope with it and even to suggest that she is impressed by Gerald's honesty. Her realisation that honesty and truth really matter show that she is capable of learning and changing. Sheila has begun to have some understanding of what the Inspector is doing so that she is able to see the world and her responsibility according to socialist values, instead of those of her capitalist family. This is why Sheila can see the trap her mother's arrogant attitude is creating and why she tries to stop her mother from exposing and condemning the child's father. In fact, at times Sheila almost seems to be the Inspector's accomplice, in that she tends to take up his criticism of other characters, even when he has left the stage. Ultimately, like the Inspector, Sheila wants to get at the truth, and she objects to her parents' attempts to protect her from unpleasant truths: '...I am not a child, don't forget. I've a right to know.'

On several occasions, Sheila shows that she can see things that the other characters cannot. She understands clearly what the Inspector is doing: 'Yes, of course it is. That's what I meant when I talked about building up a wall that's sure to be knocked flat. It makes it all harder to bear.' Sheila uses the metaphor of a wall that the Inspector will knock down to show her insightful understanding of his methods. She knows that if they try to keep anything from him, it will make things worse. The other characters don't realise this as quickly as Sheila does.

It is only Sheila and Eric, the two youngest and 'more impressionable' characters who believe everyone needs to learn something from what has happened. Sheila does seem to have learnt something and appears to have changed and we feel that her future attitude to others will be more caring, self-controlled and responsible. During the play she sees her father exposed as a hard-hearted employer, her fiancé as a liar who has had a 'kept woman,' her brother as the father of an illegitimate unborn child, her mother as cold-hearted and uncaring and herself as a vain and spiteful girl, and she is therefore forced to re-evaluate everything and everyone she has known.

Sheila as a metaphor for the younger generation

Sheila and Eric represent the younger generation which Priestley hopes is still open-minded enough to accept responsibility for others. The character of Sheila, like Eric, allows Priestley to show his opinions on youth. He felt that there was hope in the young people of post-war Britain. He saw them as the ones who would help solve the problems the country had with class, gender and social responsibility. This is seen in how Sheila is deeply affected by Eva Smith's death. She accepts responsibility straight away and promises to never behave in such a way again. This is not the case with the older characters. Mr and Mrs Birling and even Gerald do not accept responsibility and we do not get the impression that they will change. Furthermore, unlike Gerald and her parents, Sheila doesn't care about a potential scandal and recognises that whether the Inspector was real or not 'doesn't much matter', and it 'doesn't make any real difference,' since 'he inspected us all right.' This then turns to bitter sarcasm when she says, 'I suppose we are all nice people now,' and attempts bravely to remind the others that whether Eva Smith's suicide was real or not, 'everything he said that happened really happened.' For Sheila, while the others may believe that 'there is nothing to be sorry for, nothing to learn,' she remembers, 'what he said, how he looked and how he made (her) feel.' Sheila is the one ray of hope at the end of the play and the audience feel sympathy for her that she will be forced to relive the events again when the next police inspector arrives as she has truly learned her lesson.

Eric Birling

Eric begins the play 'downstage' from his parents, usually a convention in the theatre indicating a lower level of status for a character; an idea that would fit neatly with his status in the Birling family. Like his father and Gerald, he is wearing 'evening dress of the period, 'tails and white ties' (clothing worn by middle and upper-class Edwardian men) which suggests that he is like the other two men; a hint perhaps that he is already on course to 'become' another Gerald and then his father, but his position on the stage perhaps foreshadows that this will not be without scandal.

Unlike his sister, Eric is awkward 'not quite at ease, half shy, half assertive.' This also suggests that though he dresses like Gerald and Mr Birling, he is still establishing himself as a man and yet to be moulded. This is further shown when he is kept out of the information about his father's possible knighthood. His immaturity and his lack of awareness of social etiquette is shown when he 'suddenly guffaws,' a clear indication that he feels uncomfortable in social situations and is unsure of how to behave. When he is questioned about this outburst, he confesses 'I felt I just had to.' He arouses the curiosity of the audience here because this is possibly an indication that he knows something about Gerald, because Sheila has just been scolding Gerald for neglecting her in favour of his work. Curiosity turns to suspicion later, when he breaks off mid-comment – he was about to say that he remembered women find clothes important. We begin to think that Eric has something to hide.

Eric is clearly 'squiffy,' or on his way to being drunk, and this shows a lack of self-control and youthfulness, something which is repeated later in the play with his dealings with Eva Smith. Priestley purposely introduces Eric in this way so that the audience realise that the events to follow will have a significant impact on his immature character.

Eric and Gerald

Ironically, however, although Eric appears to lack the sophistication that comes with age, both he and Sheila are much more self-aware about social responsibility than their parents or Gerald, as we see in their responses to the Inspector and how they and others treated Eva Smith. At the start of the play, he may be perceived as young and immature, but events allow him to grow and become the kind of responsible man that neither Gerald nor his father ever were. In this way, Priestley both compares and juxtaposes him with Gerald:

- Both are young and set to become businessmen like their fathers.

- Both met Eva in the Palace Bar, a place associated with alcohol and the sexual exploitation of women.

- Both men have a hatred for prostitutes and objectify women 'I hate those hard doe-eyed women,' Gerald says.

- Both show hypocrisy when they pick up Daisy Renton because she appeared not to be the 'usual sort' of woman to be found at the bar.

Where the two young men differ is that Gerald is already set in his ways; he, like Birling, has become a hard-headed businessman who cares little for his workers. Eric drinks too much, has forced his way into a girl's home, has made Eva Smith pregnant and stolen money but he clearly changes as the play progresses and deeply regrets his behaviour.

Eric's relationship with his father

During the first two Acts, Eric's role is to irritate and infuriate Mr Birling, continually asking what his father regards as silly questions. Mr Birling thinks that his son has not benefited from the expensive education he has given him, perhaps because it was given to him to improve his son's status rather than develop him as a person.

Eric does not seem to have his father's affection or approval, and when he really needed help, he felt his father was 'not the kind of father a chap could go to when he's in trouble.' Eric clearly finds his father unapproachable and unloving. This may be why Eva Smith treated Eric as if he were a child and why he responded to her pity. She may have recognised in him a need for affection which she herself shared.

Eric and Eva Smith

Eric, like Sheila, feels sympathy for Eva Smith as soon as he hears how Birling had fired her. When he must admit how he behaved towards her, he has a stronger sense of guilt than the others because the consequences of what he did are so much worse. We can imagine how frightening he might have seemed to Eva Smith when he was drunk as he was 'in that state when a chap easily turns nasty.' His immaturity shows in his casual attitude towards his relationship with her. He regarded her as a 'good sport' although she treated him like a child. It is not surprising that he turns violently on his mother when he learns how she had refused to help Eva Smith: (Stage Direction: nearly at breaking point) 'You killed her – and the child she'd have had too – my child – your own grandchild.' It is only after her death that Eric understands the consequences of his relationship with Eva Smith and he is deeply regretful of this.

Eric's redemption

Eric is one of only two characters who have been impressed by the Inspector; the other being Sheila. Eric might be a weak and lonely character, but he is capable of real feelings for others. He wants his parents to admit their mistakes as freely as he admitted his. Although he is not a particularly pleasant character, we feel that he has learnt a lesson and that he is sincerely ashamed of his behaviour and can change for the better.

Despite what we know about Eric's past, he is a character who redeems himself. He sees that 'It's still the same rotten story whether it's been told to a police inspector or to somebody else…It's what happened to the girl and what we all did to her that matters.' Like Sheila, Eric is not focussed on how this will look to others, but is deeply affected by his past behaviour and is willing to change.

J.B. Priestley uses Eric as he does Sheila – to suggest that the young people of post-war Britain could be the answer to a hopeful future. With Eric, he also addresses some concerns he had about the dangers of antisocial behaviour such as excessive drinking and loss of self-control and its consequences. Priestley shows that excessive drinking and casual relationships can have negative consequences.

Gerald Croft

Gerald is the son of Birling's rival, wealthy businessman, Sir George Croft. He has the self-confidence of someone who is at ease wherever he is or whomever he is with. At the start of the play he seems very comfortable by making himself at home and behaving like a member of the Birling family. He even makes fun of Eric: 'Sure to be, unless Eric's been up to something', and he is polite and respectful towards Mr and Mrs Birling. In the stage directions, Gerald is seated next to his fiancée Sheila, a symbolic physical closeness that disappears as soon as the Inspector arrives. He is an 'attractive chap, rather too manly to be a dandy*, but very much the easy well-bred, young man-about-town,' we are told. It is not difficult to see how and why Sheila is attracted to him nor why she bitterly refers to him later in the play as 'the wonderful Fairy Prince,' who seduced and exploited Daisy Renton.

Being about thirty, he is older than Sheila and Eric whose parents treat Gerald as an equal. He is therefore a character midway between the younger two Birlings and their parents. He is trusted with the secret about Birling's possible knighthood and his views on how business should be run, how workers should be treated and the importance of profit are all in line with those of Mr Birling. Moreover, he supports Eva Smith's firing from the firm: 'You couldn't have done anything else,' he says. Gerald Croft is an outsider to the Birling family, and this allows Priestley to demonstrate that the prejudice, jealousy and dehumanising treatment of the working-classes (particularly of women) are not simply issues within the Birling family but are widespread among the middle and upper-classes of the time.

Gerald growing into his father / Arthur Birling

In his early conversations with Birling, Gerald is seen as being a bit sycophantic* in agreeing with or supporting everything Arthur Birling says:

- He says the gathering is 'much nicer really' than a big party.

- He is a 'lucky man' for marrying Sheila.

- He compliments Birling on the choice of port and then admits that he 'doesn't know much about it.'

In each instance he agrees with what is being said, showing either that he is just polite, or he is very keen to make a good impression with the Birlings. Like Birling he has had some experience of running a business:

- He knows that the young workers 'will be broke after the holidays.'
- He agrees with Birling that he 'couldn't have done anything else,' but fire Eva Smith from the factory, preventing the working-class from 'asking for the earth.'
- He comments that 'we'd have done the same.'

Gerald also seems more concerned with pleasing his future father-in-law rather than his future wife and in this way, he is an example of a patriarchal* society in action. Perhaps this is Priestley's way of suggesting that Gerald Croft is another Arthur Birling in the making.

Sympathy for Gerald

When he first meets Daisy Renton, he saves her from the awkward situation with Alderman Meggarty and sets out to help her. He had found Daisy attractive from the start and he allowed his feelings for her to develop. He felt affection for her but admits that her feelings for him were stronger than his for her. He felt guilty about only being able to offer her temporary help and when he left her, he gave her money to help her start a new life. The fact that he, 'made her happy for a time,' allows us to feel some sympathy for him. He did not treat her in the drunken way Eric did and he was probably the least to blame for her death. At first, when the truth comes out about his affair with Daisy Renton, he tries to avoid the subject: 'All right. I knew her. Let's leave it at that.' This abrupt response shows how initially Gerald is very vague about his involvement with Daisy Renton and wants to close down the topic as soon as possible. His regret for the way he used her seems genuine. He does not, however, have the same deep response as Sheila to the Inspector's message about responsibility. In fact, like Mr and Mrs Birling, his first impulse is to hide his involvement with Eva. He acts on his suspicions and as a result he is the one who begins to suspect that perhaps the Inspector is not whom he claims to be.

Gerald eventually gains some respect from Sheila and the audience for being honest about his affair: 'The girl saw me looking at her and then gave me a glance that was nothing less than a cry for help.' Gerald honestly tells the story of how he met Eva Smith. He was in the wrong to have an affair and then abandon Eva but his use of emotive language 'cry for help' makes us realise that he genuinely felt sorry for her and wanted to help her. Does Gerald feel remorse at the end of the play? He seems to expect Sheila to accept the engagement ring again and insists that all is well again.

Gerald and the upper-class

Priestley uses Gerald to attack the upper-classes of post-war Britain. He shows that despite outward appearances, (Gerald is described as an 'attractive chap' and 'well-bred') this class of people was still capable of irresponsible, improper behaviour. Perhaps Priestley is suggesting that even people of Gerald's generation have been too influenced by the older generation and are unlikely to see the need for change.

Eva Smith

Eva Smith never appears on stage, but the play revolves around the last two years of her life. It is even unclear that she is a single character and not a combination of various working-class women whom the Birlings had dealings with. Even her name 'Eva' is symbolic – coming from Eve, the first woman in the Bible, a woman who can be conveniently blamed for tempting men, a woman representing all women down the ages. From the very beginning, she is presented as being a symbol. The

Inspector describes her as being like 'a lot of these young women.' Smith too is a very common name and is certainly a working-class name by origin, a name given to those skilled at working with metal, for example, a name to symbolise perhaps a shift from rural to urban factory work. In the play, Birling mentions that Eva was brought up in the country but moved to the city.

If the name 'Eva' was meant to be symbolic, then the name Daisy Renton too would appear to be significant. It was common among prostitutes at the time to use pseudonyms* and to replace their real names with names of flowers such as rose, buttercup or daisy. The term 'flower-seller' was even used in London to mean 'prostitute.' Furthermore, the choice of the surname Renton, suggests temporary work, a person for hire.

Eva, in the words of the Inspector is presented as being the opposite of the Birlings. Unlike the Birlings, she had:

- 'no home to go back to.'
- 'both her parents were dead.'
- she had, 'no relatives to help her, few friends.'
- she was 'half-starved' and 'desperate.'

Seen through the eyes of the Birlings, she merely fulfils a function as a worker, shop assistant and sexual partner.

By the end of the play she is as familiar to us as any other character. We know she was pretty (enough to make Sheila jealous) and to attract both Gerald and Eric. She was lively and intelligent and about twenty-four years of age, roughly the same as Sheila. Eva Smith shows that she is strong-willed when she organises a strike for higher wages. This demonstrates that she is not afraid to stand up to 'hard-headed' businessmen like Mr Birling.

We learn about her hard life and unpleasant death, and this contrasts sharply with what we see and learn of the Birling and Croft families. She worked hard, supported her fellow workers and was kind and gentle. Although she was reduced to picking up men in the Palace Theatre Bar, she did not seem suited to that way of life. Eva shows that she has a sense of humour when she smiles as Sheila tries on a dress that doesn't suit her. The audience warms to Eva and sees her as human.

Her understanding of right and wrong prevented her from considering marriage to Eric and she protected him when he stole money from the firm. Despite five separate stories concerning Eva, she remains more of a symbol than a real person. Furthermore, the diary Eva kept after her affair with Gerald ended shows that she felt emotions very deeply and the audience empathises with her as a result. The Inspector explains how Eva Smith went away to be 'quiet' and to 'remember.' These words clearly show that Eva was emotionally sensitive. The fact that she also felt that 'there'd never be anything as good again for her' make us realise how devastated she was when Gerald ended their relationship; that Gerald just got back on with his life and with Sheila makes the audience sympathise even more with the sensitive Eva Smith.

How Eva Smith was treated

It is worth considering briefly what each of the Birlings and Gerald take from her:

- Birling destroys her social status and takes her away from the group of which she was a member by firing her.

- Sheila destroys her chances of a paid job to the point where she doesn't even 'feel like trying' for a new job.
- Gerald takes a genuine interest in her but after leaving her, damages her emotionally.
- Eric abuses her.
- Mrs Birling rejects her.

Each incident illustrates that Eva Smith is easy prey for 'respectable' society. We can track her journey through the play in terms of the names she chooses:

- To Birling she was Eva Smith.
- To Sheila she was an anonymous shop assistant, whose name she didn't even bother to learn.
- To Gerald and Eric, she was Daisy Renton.
- To Sybil Birling, she was Mrs Birling.

Ironically, as her circumstances get worse, she seems to become more honourable, which contrasts with the other characters. We see a hopeful young life destroyed by the selfishness and thoughtlessness of others. She stands for all the different people we meet in our everyday lives. Priestley uses her tragedy to jolt us into thinking about our responsibility towards other people. She is the instrument the Inspector uses to try to change society.

Edna

Edna, the maid, appears only briefly; however, she serves as an important, symbolic function in the play. She is evidence of the privilege and wealth of the Birlings, (only certain classes could afford domestic help in the home). It is noticeable that we are given very little information about Edna – she is simply described as 'the parlour maid' in the stage directions.

Edna is given no distinguishing features, no age, no accent – nothing. She is largely ignored by the family, not even thanked by Mr Birling for bringing him the port. She is defined by her role as a servant and as such, she is not considered. It is only when Edna leaves the room that Birling can relax. This could suggest that the family are made to feel a little uncomfortable by the presence of a 'working-class' woman in the household. Perhaps she is an unwanted reminder to Arthur Birling of his working-class upbringing and of the workers he exploits in his factory?

It is Edna who is asked for 'more light' in the room and who announces the arrival of the Inspector – a character who in turn will shed light on the Birlings' behaviour and family secrets.

Her brief appearance on stage and her general absence from the events in the play may also act as a reminder to the audience of the Birlings' ignorance and dismissal of the working-class.

Progress and revision check

1. What various roles does the Inspector have in the play?

2. In what way is the family home a metaphor for Arthur Birling?

3. What evidence is there to suggest that Birling has not been a good parent?

4. How is Mrs Birling shown to be a hypocrite?

5. How is Sheila presented at the beginning of the play?

6. Give an example of how Sheila increasingly challenges her parents as the play progresses.

7. In what way is Eric shown to be immature and lacking in social etiquette?

8. What sort of relationship does Eric have with his father?

9. In what ways is Gerald shown to be more like Arthur Birling and his father than Eric?

10. How is Eva Smith presented as being the opposite to the Birlings and Gerald?

~ Themes ~

Social responsibility

The play was first performed in Britain just after the end of World War Two in 1946. It was a time of great change in Britain and many writers were concerned with the welfare of the poor. At that time there was no financial support for people like Eva Smith who could not afford to look after themselves. Priestley wanted to address this issue. He also felt that if people were more considerate of one another, it would improve quality of life for all. This is why social responsibility is a key theme of the play. Priestley wanted his audience to be responsible for their own behaviour and responsible for the welfare of others.

The Inspector and social responsibility

It is no surprise that Inspector Goole (generally accepted as Priestley's mouthpiece in the play) uses his final speech to reinforce the key idea of social responsibility: 'We are members of one body,' he tells the Birlings, personifying society and using language with a clear reference to the Christian rite of communion. 'We are responsible for each other. We do not live alone,' he says. This perhaps is the most important and central theme of the play: we have a duty and responsibility to other people, regardless of social status, wealth, class or anything else. Priestley reinforces this by having the Inspector constantly repeating the collective pronoun 'we'. There is, Priestley observes, such a thing as society, and he argues that it is important that people be aware of the effects of their actions on others. The Birlings initially do not think at all about how they might have affected Eva Smith, but they are forced to confront their responsibility over the course of the play.

This sense of social responsibility is key to understanding the Inspector's role within the play: he is not there just to investigate Eva's suicide, but to force the Birling family to admit they failed Eva Smith and others like her and to take responsibility for their actions. In Act Two, for example, when Mrs Birling insists to the Inspector that 'I don't think we need discuss it,' he stresses that 'you have no hope of not discussing it, Mrs Birling,' agreeing with Sheila earlier in the Act that 'we have to share something. If there's nothing else, we'll have to share our guilt.' What Priestley is saying is that individuals in society do not live alone and cannot avoid their social responsibility towards others.

The Birlings' idea of responsibility

Each of the Birlings and Gerald have a key responsibility to society and others, however, they do not use it wisely:

- Mr Birling is a businessman and as such he feels his responsibility is to make a success of his business which means making as much profit as possible, even if that results in being harsh with those who work for him. As a family man he sees that he has a responsibility to provide for the material needs of his family, yet Eric does not see him as 'the kind of father' to whom he could turn when in trouble.

- Mrs Birling accepts her responsibility as chairwoman of the Women's Charity Organization but only sees a responsibility to help those that she feels deserve it.

- Sheila recognises that, as a powerful customer, she has an obligation not to let her feelings and bad temper lead to misery for people who have no power.

- Eric has little sense of responsibility. He drinks far more than is good for him and he forces Eva into a relationship which has disastrous consequences.

- Gerald shows some sense of responsibility when he rescues Eva from the unwanted attention of another man, feeds her and finds her somewhere to live. Yet he gives in to his own desire for personal pleasure and abandons her without knowing or caring what happens to her.

Each of the Birlings attempts to hide their responsibility or avoid discussing it: Birling cuts off Eric when he tries to repeat his father's comments and denies knowing anything about Eva, despite later remembering Eva in some detail; both Sheila and Eric simply leave the room, or the house (in Eric's case), though they later return to confront their actions; and Mrs Birling refuses to even consider the possibility of her being responsible:

- 'I don't think we can help you much.'
- 'I don't know what you're talking about.'
- 'I don't suppose for a moment that we can understand why.'
- 'I don't see any particular reason,' she claims in Act Two.
- 'I don't understand you.'
- 'I don't know anything about this girl.'

It is only Gerald, however, who actively attempts to deceive the Inspector, 'don't say anything to the inspector,' he begs Sheila at the end of Act One, 'we can keep it from him.'

Instead of fulfilling their responsibility and helping those to whom they have a duty, they choose to look after themselves, and this is what Priestley is criticising.

Reactions to their social responsibility

Birling is so concerned about public opinion and his fear of public disgrace that he is unable to see the seriousness of what has happened:

- He jokes to Gerald in Act One that his main fear is of getting 'into the police court' or starting 'a scandal'.
- He is worried about his wife's refusal to help Eva Smith coming 'out at the inquest' since 'The Press might easily take it up.'
- As self-centred as ever, Birling is concerned that the whole story 'isn't going to do us much good.'
- Even after being 'terrified' to learn that Eric is involved, as the stage direction tells us, Birling focuses almost entirely on his son's theft from the company, determined to 'cover this up' in order to avoid the 'public scandal', preventing him from 'a knighthood in the next Honours List', which he tells Eric in Act Three.

Mrs Birling's reactions to learning about Eric's affair with Daisy Renton also shows that she has not learned the lesson of responsibility: 'I should think not. Eric, I'm absolutely ashamed of you.' By saying this to Eric, she shows that she has learned nothing from the Inspector's investigation. The audience would know that she is in no position to be questioning the behaviour of anyone else given her own treatment of Eva Smith and her lack of social responsibility.

Forced to look ashamed in public may be the worst that can happen to Birling but for Eric and Sheila, 'it's what happened to the girl and what we all did to her that matters.' They acknowledge that they bear some responsibility for what happened to Eva Smith. Sheila is one character who has learnt the lesson about responsibility and she is genuinely shocked to learn of her part in Eva's death. 'All right Gerald, you needn't look at me like that. At least I'm trying to tell the truth.' Here Sheila tells the truth as a way to take responsibility for her actions, despite the fact she can't change them.

Eric also takes responsibility for his actions in the final Act of the play. 'I don't see much nonsense about it when a girl goes and kills herself. You lot may be letting yourselves out nicely, but I can't. Nor can mother. We did her in all right.' Eric clearly shows that he has a sense of social responsibility. Whilst Eric's parents and Gerald are enjoying being in the clear, Eric still takes the matter of Eva's death very seriously. He is even brave enough to tell his mother that she should feel responsible too.

What Priestley seems to be suggesting through the play is that the moral – how we behave – is more important than whether a crime has been committed or not. For Priestley, the story acts as a metaphor for both the problems in society and the actions needed to solve them. Though responsibility is a major theme of the play, the last Act provides a fascinating portrait of the way that people can let themselves off the hook. If one message of the play is that we must all care more about the general welfare of others, the message is not shared by all. By contrasting the older Birlings and Gerald with Sheila and Eric, Priestley explicitly draws out the difference between those who have accepted their responsibility and those who have not; those who are prepared to listen and learn and those who are not.

The Inspector's final speech

The Inspector's parting words are very important because they sum up the main message of the play and Priestley's own socialist views. There are three key sections to consider:

Firstly, he says, 'One Eva Smith has gone…intertwined with our lives.' Here Priestley is highlighting that Eva Smith is a symbol: a representation of all other poor citizens in the community. The story has not finished with her death, as there are millions of other men and women who need looking after in society and it is essential that we all take responsibility for our actions towards them, including those less fortunate than ourselves. The surname 'Smith' and the name 'John' were some of the most common in the country and this again suggests that they stand for other, less advantaged people in our society.

This section is followed by possibly the most important line in the play: 'We don't live alone. We are members of one body – we are responsible for each other.' In these few words, Priestley sums up his message about social responsibility not only to Gerald and the Birlings, but to the audience and wider society. They also remind us of Jesus Christ's words to his disciples at The Last Supper suggesting that all people, regardless of their class, wealth or status share a common humanity.

The final part of the speech contains a warning for those unwilling to accept this message of social responsibility: 'The time will soon come when…fire, blood and anguish.' The words 'fire, blood and anguish' have at least two possible interpretations. They appear in the Bible in reference to Hell and the end of the world. Therefore, one meaning of these words could be that if people are unwilling to take responsibility for each other here on earth, then they will be sent to Hell to learn the lesson there. This interpretation fits in well with the idea that the Inspector is a ghoul, or a spirit sent from God to warn those on earth of the consequences of their actions if they don't learn to take responsibility for their behaviour. Alternatively, the phrase could refer to war since 'fire, blood and anguish' are words that have reference to violent conflict. The

Inspector may be warning both the Birlings and the audience that if men and women refuse to look after one another, more wars and conflicts may follow, like the Second World War, which the 1946 audience would have just lived through.

The Inspector's final words are different in both tone and delivery to his other statements in the play. This is clearly a speech not a conversation and is therefore aimed not only at the Birlings but at the audience as well. Although brief, it has the features of a speech:

- Note the way he begins: 'But just remember this.' The Inspector wants his last words to stay with us and leave the theatre with the audience.
- He uses repetition and exaggeration, both key characteristics of a speech to hammer home his point: 'millions and millions and millions of Eva Smiths and John Smiths...'
- He goes on to mention all the things that humans share and feel that bind us together: 'hopes and fears,' 'suffering and chances of happiness all intertwined,' to appeal to the Birlings and his audience for collective social responsibility and welfare for all.
- His speech, like a sermon from the pulpit or an address at a political rally, ends with a warning if his words and message are ignored, 'They will be taught it in fire, blood and anguish.'

The Inspector's final words sound nothing like those of a normal policeman and perhaps it is these words more than any others that make Gerald and Birling suspect that he was not a real inspector. The audience too, will notice that his speech feels and sounds different; that perhaps this was Priestley's opportunity to metaphorically 'step onto the stage' and deliver his most important message of the play.

Love and marriage

The play presents a variety of ideas about love and marriage and different people's beliefs about love. Sheila and Gerald appear to be in love; they have just announced their engagement and seem to be happy to spend the rest of their lives together. After each of them has confessed to their shameful behaviour towards Eva Smith, Sheila realises that they do not really know each other well and that trust is an essential ingredient in a loving relationship.

Mr Birling's remark about the engagement of his daughter bringing the firms into a closer working relationship gives us an understanding of his attitude towards love and marriage. He sees marriage as a convenient way of progressing up the social and economic ladder. This makes us wonder whether love played any part in his marriage to the socially superior Sybil Birling. It also makes us question whether her coldness to others, including her own two children, is because she is in a loveless marriage.

Both Gerald and Eric have been involved with Eva Smith yet each of them denies that they loved her – their relationships were driven purely by physical attraction. Eva had started a relationship with Eric out of necessity, but she does seem to have felt genuine love for Gerald. Gerald's ending of the affair therefore may be seen as being cruel considering her feelings for him.

The Inspector preaches a form of love like Jesus Christ's when he instructed his followers to love one another as much as they love themselves. This form of love, Priestley may be suggesting, is the sort of love everyone should practise towards others in society. It is a form of love that is quite alien to women like Mrs Birling, who carry out voluntary work for local charities but have no real love in their hearts for other people less fortunate than themselves. Therefore, several kinds of love are depicted in the play:

- The love between a husband and wife.

- The romantic love of Gerald and Sheila.

- The unrequited love of Eva for Gerald – she cared for him in a way that was not returned by him.

- The lustful love of Eric for Eva Smith which resulted in a pregnancy.

- The love of parents for their children and the family love between brother and sister.

- The Inspector's love of truth.

Priestley is perhaps questioning these different expressions of human love and asks the audience to decide how real they are.

Social class

Before World War Two, Britain was divided by class. Two such classes were the wealthy land and factory owners (the upper-classes) and the poor workers (the working-class). The Second World War helped bring these two classes closer together and rationing meant that people of all classes were eating and even dressing the same. This also meant that people from all classes were mixing together. This was certainly not the case before. Priestley wanted to highlight that inequality between the classes still existed however and that the upper-classes and middle-classes looked down upon the working-class in post-war Britain.

The Birling family are carefully set up in order to act as a microcosm* of the middle-class. We have the older generation and the younger with both genders represented in each. We have the rising middle-class in the self-made businessman Arthur Birling, and the more established middle-class in Mrs Birling. There is the blending of the middle-class and the upper-class through the relationship with Gerald Croft and finally those who have inherited their wealth from their parents: Sheila, Eric and Gerald.

Mrs Birling looks down on people from 'inferior' classes as we see in her comment about Eva Smith: 'As if a girl of that sort would ever refuse money!' Mrs Birling refers to Eva Smith as a 'girl of that 'sort'. She clearly has prejudiced views about working-class girls suggesting that they lack morals and will always take money.

The Inspector suggests that he doesn't believe in class division: 'We are members of one body.' This metaphor of the 'body' suggests that class division should not exist as everyone in the world is one society. It also has connotations of a human body, because if one part of the body, such as the heart, was to stop working the whole body would shut down. This links to the Birlings because if one of them stops caring about the lower class, others will follow. The pronoun 'we' suggests that the Inspector is addressing everyone together as they all have a part to play.

Gender

For Mr Birling, Gerald and Eric, there is the clear view that men and women have not been created as equals. For Birling, working-class women are all the same: 'We've several hundred young women', Birling tells the Inspector, 'and they keep changing.' Gerald and Eric share a similar prejudice in terms of their hatred for 'those hard-eyed, dough-faced women', as Gerald calls them. To both men, all the women who hang out at the Palace Hotel are the same.

The gender balance is important. Both men and women are to blame in terms of collective responsibility for the evils of the class system, though their sins are very different. Sheila and Mrs Birling simply dismiss Eva Smith without thought because of jealousy or prejudice. Birling exploits her social weakness and Eric and Gerald exploit her sexually and socially (she is in a lower class to them) making use of her body.

For both Sheila and Mrs Birling, there is a lack of empathy. Although all three share the same gender, for Mrs Birling and Sheila, being of the same class is more important. This is despite Sheila's assertion that 'these girls aren't cheap labour – they're people.' The Inspector is particularly damning of Mrs Birling in Act Two: 'She came to you for help, at a time when no woman could have needed it more', he tells her, 'you've had children. You must have known what she was feeling.' The Inspector here suggests that being both a woman and a mother, Mrs Birling should have had more empathy for the young, pregnant Eva Smith.

Birling, Eric and Gerald all judge Eva because of her appearance:

- Birling describes her in Act One as a 'lively, good-looking girl', which has nothing to do with her role within his company.
- Gerald notices her because she is 'very pretty', 'young and fresh and charming.'
- Eric notices her because she 'wasn't the usual sort', and because she was 'pretty.'
- Even the Inspector, in Act One, admits that she was 'pretty – very pretty.'

Perhaps Sheila's involvement with Eva Smith is linked to this idea of her appearance; that women are defined by what their men want them to look like. After all, Sheila goes to Milwards at least partially for Gerald's benefit, she admits to him in Act One, and is jealous of Eva because she is 'very pretty' and because she feels that she herself looks 'awful' in the dress. Had Eva been 'some miserable plain little creature', it may never have happened, she admits. Perhaps had her fiancée been more attentive and had less of a wandering eye, Sheila may not have felt so insecure. The vulnerability of women in Edwardian and post-World War Two society, evokes sympathy, which supports Priestley's belief in gender equality and community as 'one body.' Priestley includes a strong range of female characters in the play from an upper-class snob through a vain daughter to an oppressed factory worker, showing he wanted to convey women from all types of social background.

Both Gerald and Eric seem to feel that men have a natural right to a woman's body. Aside from their shallow view of Eva Smith and their disgust at the women that they seem to spend time with and take advantage of, Gerald sees his relationship with Eva as being 'inevitable' since she was 'young and pretty and warm-hearted – and intensely grateful.' Eric 'insisted' on going back to her lodgings even though 'she didn't want me to', excusing his actions since he was 'in that state when a chap easily turns nasty' and of course sex with her was acceptable since she was 'pretty and a good sport.'

There is an assumption underlying the behaviour of Eric and Gerald that this is a 'normal' thing. Birling, after all, 'broke out and had a bit of fun sometimes' when he was younger, while the lifestyle of couples such as Birling and Mrs Birling, with the lack of romantic intimacy visible from the beginning of the play, is something that Sheila will simply 'have to get used to,' as Mrs Birling did. Even after the full version of Gerald's story has been revealed, Birling still attempts to convince Sheila that she 'must understand that a lot of young men -' before being interrupted by his daughter. Priestley is exposing the male belief that women could be taken advantage of and he criticises this through the treatment of Eva Smith, and to an extent Sheila, who the audience feel sympathy for because of the way they were treated by men.

In the play, to be a woman is:

- to be defined by your relationship with your male family members.

- to be viewed and judged by your appearance rather than evaluated in terms of your abilities or personal qualities.

- to be forced to accept the gender roles that society offers you.

It is these very stereotypes that Priestley is hoping to change through this play.

Young and old

The play draws out a significant contrast between the older and younger generations of Birlings. The older characters' opinions and behaviour are stubbornly fixed. While Arthur and Sybil refuse to accept responsibility for their actions towards Eva Smith (Arthur is only concerned for his reputation and his potential knighthood), Eric and especially Sheila are shaken by the Inspector's message and their role in Eva Smith's suicide. They accept their mistakes and offer a chance for a brighter future. The younger generation is taking more responsibility, perhaps because they are more emotional and have hopes for the future.

Writing as he was during the Second World War and having seen active service himself, Priestley knew the younger generation had suffered significantly during the First World War only to return to a country where there were few jobs for young people. A phrase commonly used for those who served and were left directionless afterwards, or for the thousands of young people killed, was the 'Lost Generation', coined by the writer Gertrude Stein. One reason the phrase caught on is because it implies a regret for the lost potential of youth wasted and killed in a senseless war.

In many ways, An Inspector Calls seems to act as a microcosm for the broader society in which Priestley lived. We see the older generation represented by Mr and Mrs Birling and by Sir George and Lady Croft, either exploiting the younger generation through Eva Smith, or misleading and negatively impacting on them in terms of Eric and Sheila.

The negative impact of the older generation on the younger and the mismatch between the generations is obvious from the beginning. Birling in his first act of the play pushes the port towards Eric, encouraging him to drink, while Mrs Birling talks down to Sheila, belittling her almost immediately in giving her marital advice: 'When you're married', she tells her, 'you'll realise that men with important work to do sometimes have to spend nearly all their time and energy on their business,' then criticising her behaviour, with 'really the things you girls pick up these days!' The noun choice is worth noting: Sheila, to Mrs Birling, is a 'girl', while Eric is consistently a 'boy' to both parents and both are grouped together as 'youngsters' by Birling in Act One. The double-standard is particularly evident when Birling describes Sheila near the beginning as a 'lucky girl' but Gerald as a 'fortunate young man,' even though his daughter is roughly the same age as Gerald. While Birling may not approve of what 'some of these boys get up to nowadays' in Act One, describing them as 'boys' seems to excuse their behaviour as simply youthful antics.

It is the Inspector who seems to show Eva Smith, Eric and Sheila some respect. Eva, not long after the Inspector first appears, is a 'young woman' rather than the 'girl' that Birling belittles her as being, while during the discussion about drinking in Act Two, Eric is, clearly, a 'young man.'

Birling consistently belittles Eric. In addition to the range of opinions he expresses in Act One, he interrupts his son, reminding him that 'You've a lot to learn yet.' For Birling, Eric is someone he needs to educate. For the audience, however, it is only too clear that Eric has only negative things to learn from his father.

In contrast, Eric appears to want to interrogate his father's views from the beginning of the play:

- He queries the possibility of war.

- He attempts to argue when his father expresses his views.

- He continues disagreeing with his father regarding opportunities for the workers and Birling's actions towards Eva Smith.

Eric is more open-minded than his father: 'Why shouldn't they try for higher wages?' he asks Birling, 'I'd have let her stay.' Eric appears, unlike Birling, not to see a real division between the classes. Sheila similarly, sees Birling's actions as 'mean,' with Eva's life being a 'rotten shame.'

Eric stands up to his parents when it becomes clear that they will not take responsibility: 'You're beginning to pretend now that nothing's really happened at all.' Eric sees that his parents are trying to 'pretend' that nothing happened when it is suggested that the Inspector was not real. He and Sheila, the younger characters, still feel responsible. Mr Birling turns on his son and nearly attacks him physically. 'Why, you hysterical young fool – get back – or I'll...' Mr Birling implies here that Eric is a 'fool' because he is young. Ironically, it is the older Arthur who nearly resorts to physical violence and has acted foolishly throughout.

It is significant that not only do the younger generation learn their lesson, but they are the only members of the Birling family that are left with any dignity at the end of the play. Priestley is once again demonstrating his hope for the future of the country and it is the younger generation, those who will be in power in the future, that have the opportunity to change society's ways.

Progress and revision check

1. In the play, who might be seen to be 'Priestley's mouthpiece'?

2. In what ways have each of the Birlings and Gerald acted irresponsibly?

3. Which of the characters learn the lesson of social responsibility? What is it that they learn?

4. At the end of the play the audience may feel that Mr and Mrs Birling have learnt nothing. Why is this?

5. Why did Birling marry Sybil?

6. What did Birling bring to his marriage with Sybil?

7. In what ways were men and women treated differently in 1912?

8. How is Eva treated as an object rather than as a person by Eric and Gerald?

9. In what ways are both Eric and Sheila still treated like children by their parents?

10. Why is Edna merely described as 'the parlour maid' in the stage directions?

~ Form, structure and language ~

Form

A play to be watched

A key starting point to be aware of is that this is a play, not a novel or a short story. Watching a play is an immediate and collective experience; we are in the moment with the characters; and we react not just to what is on stage, but also to the responses of those around us.

A play is very different to a novel; rather than fixed words on a page that we interpret on our own terms as individual readers, theatrical performances are interactive; we, as an audience, have no control over when they begin or end; we observe from a third person perspective, outsiders and witnesses; and actors make different choices in their acting each night that makes each performance unique.

A script is also more open to interpretation than a novel. After all, the writer's words, including the all-important stage directions, are interpreted by a director and the actors, and this then helps the audience to understand the play. When Sheila, for example, brings up Gerald ignoring her the previous summer, the exact balance between 'playful' and 'serious' must be decided by the director and the actor: did Sheila really understand what was happening that summer? It is the director and actor who decide that, not the reader.

The production can also use aspects such as lighting, sound, set design, costume and props to emphasise key aspects. At the beginning of the play, for example, Priestley advises that the lighting should be 'pink and intimate', becoming 'brighter and harder' when the Inspector arrives, to reflect the shift from cosy pretences (like rose-tinted glasses) to the harsher lights of the interrogation that the Inspector will conduct.

A morality play

The play is also like a traditional morality play. Morality plays were popular during the 15th and 16th centuries. They were written to teach the audience lessons that focused on the seven deadly sins: lust*, gluttony*, greed, sloth*, wrath*, envy and pride*. Whilst characters who committed these sins were punished, morality plays showed that if a character admitted their mistakes, they could be saved. An Inspector Calls is a morality play because the Birlings and Gerald Croft commit 'crimes' which are similar to the seven deadly sins:

- Mr Birling is greedy because he wants more money.
- Sheila is guilty of wrath and envy when she spitefully complains about Eva Smith.
- Eric and Gerald are guilty of lust when they sexually abuse Eva Smith.
- Mrs Birling is too proud to help someone less fortunate than herself.

But do all the characters redeem themselves?

Priestley uses the form of a morality play to teach a 20th century audience a series of lessons that relate to his beliefs about social responsibility, age, gender and class. The audience is invited to enjoy judging these characters, but they are also forced to question their own behaviour. Priestley would have hoped that people watching the play would have left the theatre as better people.

A crime thriller

The play is also written like a crime thriller. The audience receives clues about who has committed the crime and will enjoy trying to guess what happened before the end of the action. An Inspector Calls is a crime thriller in another sense because the action centres around the suicide of Eva Smith. Initially, as this is a suicide and not a murder investigation, there is no clear suspect. It soon turns out that all the characters are potential suspects for different reasons and like a traditional crime thriller, all had a part to play in her death.

The crime thriller form encourages the audience to become involved in the events of the play. In this case they would be considering who is 'more' to blame for the death of Eva Smith. Ultimately, Priestley makes the audience suspects, their behaviour is questioned, and they are left wondering if they had committed any social 'crimes' like the Birlings did.

Structure

The well-made play

The drama unfolds in one place – the Birlings' dining room. The action is straightforward, without any complicating subplots, and events in the play take up about the same amount of time as passes in the theatre. The breaks between acts do not disturb the action of the play and are not used to change the setting. Even when there is a break between acts when an interval might take place, the start of the next Act takes us to the same place and time as before. This makes the action of the play realistic and convincing, concentrates the attention of the audience and makes the ending more surprising. All this makes for what 19th century dramatists called 'a well-made play.' The plot is complicated and complex and builds to a final climax. This structure allows Priestley to manipulate the audience. The audience do not know what happened to Eva Smith and so each revelation about her treatment by the Birlings and Gerald Croft adds to the drama. Each revelation is more shocking than the last and so Priestley cleverly builds to the climax. In An Inspector Calls there is a twist at the end of the plot – the characters are unsure if the Inspector existed at all. This gives the audience time to reflect on the events of the play. When it is revealed that another inspector is on his way and the curtain falls, the audience would be stunned into questioning their own morals and whether their behaviour could also be 'inspected'.

The Inspector's use of questioning

The action is taken forward by the Inspector's questioning of each character in turn. Their reasons for entering and leaving the stage are always believable and always allow some new part of the plot to be introduced or something that was mentioned earlier to be developed. The play is built up in a series of episodes and each character has either a leading or supporting role in each of these episodes, even in their absence. Gerald's decision to go for a walk, for example, means that he can change the course of events after the Inspector's departure, while Eric's absence allows his involvement with Eva Smith to be explored in a way that could not be if he was present.

Each new revelation, prompted by the Inspector's careful use of the photograph or information from the diary, adds to the overall picture of those two crucial years in Eva Smith's life. Each part fits together and helps to complete the jigsaw of events. As the pattern develops the audience can predict what will happen next. By making the Inspector's line of questioning a key element of the structure, Priestley cleverly allows the audience to realise the power that he has over the Birlings and Gerald.

Changing moods

The play begins in a mood of high celebration but after the Inspector's entrance, the other characters have little reason to be pleased with themselves and the mood becomes serious, even threatening. By the time the Inspector delivers his final speech the mood has become one that promises real danger for the future. The relief that is felt when Gerald says the Inspector is not real and no evidence of a suicide can be found, is shattered by the dramatic telephone call.

Plot twists

Although the action and time span of the play is realistic, Priestley introduces two twists at the end. Firstly, we have the question of who the Inspector really is: a trickster determined to make fools of them, or a spirit who has come to make them see the error of their ways? The second twist is when the telephone call interrupts the characters and takes them back to relive the events. It is this which allows the possibility that the Inspector is a real policeman who has slipped out of real time and will return. If they fail to learn from their experiences and are 'ready to go on in the same old way,' the Inspector's threat of 'fire and blood and anguish' might become their reality. Priestley is reminding his audience that history will repeat itself if they do not learn their lesson.

Language

Priestley has written the play in realistic style; all of the characters speak in the way that they would have done in 1912.

Dashes and interruptions

Priestley uses dashes and interruptions throughout the play. As in normal conversation:

- Characters hesitate.
- They self-interrupt and interrupt each other.
- They fail to complete sentences.
- They speak in strings of sentence fragments, typically conveyed through Priestley's trademark use of dashes.

It is noticeable that when characters are feeling comfortable and confident, as at the beginning of the play, there are few interruptions and sentences are typically long and grammatically complete. Where characters are upset or scared, the reverse is true. As an effective example of this, compare Birling's speeches at the beginning of Act One with Eric's just before the departure of the Inspector in Act Three.

Interruptions too are important in helping an audience follow changing relationships between the characters. They show the shifting of power and influence between the characters as the play progresses. Birling, throughout Act One, interrupts characters in order to assert his dominance, particularly Eric and the Inspector. It's noticeable that by Act Three, it is Birling who is interrupted by Sheila, the Inspector and Eric; the characters who have gained the most influence and have changed the most as the plot has developed.

Euphemisms

There is also a shift in terms of the use of euphemisms* in the play. Almost anything that is seen as being rude, vulgar or harsh is euphemised:

- Eric is 'squiffy' rather than drunk both at the beginning and when he met Eva.

- Eva was 'discharged' by Birling rather than being fired or sacked.

- Birling assumes that Eva had to 'go on the streets', a euphemism for homelessness or prostitution.

- Gerald was 'seeing' Eva rather than having an affair, a relationship or simply having sex with her.

- Gerald detests 'women of the town' rather than referring to them as prostitutes.

- Eric uses a euphemism when he tells his family and the Inspector in Act Three that 'it happened', when referring to having sex with Eva Smith or the strong implication that he forced himself upon her.

Euphemisms are an attempt to disguise the seriousness of an action or event. Note that the Inspector doesn't use them, and neither does Sheila: they tell the truth and say things as they are. By Birling, Gerald and Eric relying on euphemisms, it is an attempt to make what they actually did sound acceptable, but the audience know that this is not the case.

Characters' individual style of speaking

Individual characters have distinct manners of speaking. Birling, quite apart from being 'rather provincial in his speech,' tends to ask rhetorical questions, almost as though he needs assurance and confirmation from people around him, which is in contrast to the confidence that he displays. Perhaps he is trying to fit into a world that he knows he did not always belong to? Birling frequently repeats himself and shifts to speech-making mode throughout the opening of the play in order to assert himself or boast about his knowledge of certain things. His contributions in the play are littered with the vocabulary of business and money, such as 'capital', 'cost' and 'profit' and he is far more likely than any other character to use the pronoun 'I', a clear reflection of his arrogance and self-centredness.

In addition to the reference to being 'her husband's social superior', suggesting a more upper-class accent, Mrs Birling is more grammatically correct and formal in what she says and far less likely than any other character to ask questions. This suggests a high degree of certainty, self-confidence and personal security, in direct contrast to her husband.

Sheila and Eric are both less confident in their use of language, and instead resort to using slang in their first few contributions. This is because they are young, less experienced in life and naive about the outside world.

Gerald seems to fall somewhere between the others: not as arrogant as Birling, but not as confident as Mrs Birling; not as insecure as Eric and Sheila, but still capable of showing emotion.

The Inspector, however, is notably different in his manner of speaking from any other character, in his use of simple, direct language. This is presumably because Priestley wanted his words to have a clear impact on the Birlings, Gerald and his audience. The Inspector uses many questions, hardly a surprise in terms of his role, though these are often direct or brief; they are more like prompts for others to express or share rather than a direct interrogation. The Inspector's questions are also balanced by offering judgements about the other characters' actions, although it is noticeable that he is far more likely than Birling to offer a straight statement such as 'it's better to ask for the earth than to take it', linked perhaps to his function as a voice of morality and society rather than being an individual.

In his final speech, the Inspector's style is also the only example of non-realistic speech in the play, with religious references such as 'we are members of one body', and 'fire blood and anguish,' an image that refers both to war and Hell. It is in his final speech that the Inspector also addresses Eva as the key symbol in the play: she is simply 'one' of 'millions and millions and millions' of working-class men and women like her. His tone and language change here because it is his last opportunity to get the message of social responsibility across.

Key images in the play

There are some recurring images in the play. Alcohol for example, seems to represent the corrupting influence of the older generation and the dangerous self-indulgence of the middle-class. It is also associated with antisocial behaviour. It is Birling who encourages others to drink at the beginning of the play. Indeed, Birling's first act in the play is to pass Eric the port and he forces his wife to drink too. Birling also offers the Inspector alcohol as soon as he arrives, something he would know to be inappropriate for a policeman on duty to accept. Alcohol is also linked to Gerald's initial approach to Daisy Renton, Eric's suggested rape of Eva and Alderman Meggarty's inappropriate behaviour.

Sheila uses the image of a wall to describe her mother's attempt to avoid responsibility and her refusal to accept the reality of what has happened, and this links neatly to both the setting and the staging. After all, it is this fourth wall that has been broken to allow us to observe the Birlings' evening, yet it is also the closed-off world of the Birlings that the Inspector is demolishing, 'a wall that's sure to be knocked flat', as Sheila describes it.

Physical space

It is noticeable that the influence the Birlings have over their world is conveyed through their control over physical spaces:

- Birling has Eva removed from his factory.
- Sheila has Eva removed from a shop.
- Gerald allows Eva access to a hotel and his friend's flat and then removes her from it.
- Eric takes away Eva's right to her own personal space by invading her lodgings and then forcing himself upon her.

Perhaps the clearest example of this is Birling's assumption in Act One that Eva, having been fired from his factory, would have to 'go on the streets': that there is no place in the world controlled by the Birlings for those like Eva.

Progress and revision check

1. What factors make the play seem realistic?

2. How does Priestley change the mood of the play by using lighting?

3. What are morality plays? In what way is the play like one?

4. How is the play like a traditional crime thriller?

5. What are euphemisms generally used for?

6. How does the way Mrs Birling speaks tell us something about her class and character?

7. What might alcohol symbolise in the play?

8. In what way is the Inspector's manner of speaking different to the other characters?

9. How does Sheila use the image of the wall?

10. In what ways do the Birlings control the 'space' (and hence the world) that Eva Smith occupies?

~ Key quotations and glossary ~

Key quotations

The Inspector

Stage direction telling us something about his appearance:

- 'an impression of massiveness, solidity and purposefulness.'

Challenges the Birlings to stop thinking about themselves and start thinking of others:

- 'well we know one young woman who wasn't (protected) against…disturbing things.'

Reveals the Inspector's influence on the younger Birlings:

- 'we often do on the young ones, they're more impressionable.'

Directly confronts Mrs Birling about her dealings with Eva Smith:

- 'I think you did something terribly wrong.'

Demonstrates his authority over the Birlings and that he is not afraid of them:

- 'Don't stammer and yammer at me again man! I am losing all patience with you people.'
- 'I know he's your son and this is your house – but look at him!'
- 'If you are easy with me, I'm easy with you.'

Voices Priestley's social message in his final speech:

- 'We do not live alone. We are members of one body.'
- 'One Eva Smith has gone...intertwined with our lives.'

- 'millions and millions and millions of Eva Smiths and John Smiths...'
- 'we are responsible for each other.'

Voices Priestley's warning if his message is not heard and people do not change:

- 'If men will not learn the lesson, then they will be taught it in fire and blood and anguish.'

Mr Birling

Stage direction telling us about the Birlings' home but also a metaphor for Birling and his wealth:

- 'heavily comfortable but not cosy.'
- 'decanter of port, cigar box and cigarettes.'

Stage directions telling us about Birling's appearance:

- 'heavy looking'
- 'portentous'

Reveals how out of touch he is with reality and the outside world:

- 'The Titanic... every luxury, unsinkable...'
- 'You will hear some people say that war is inevitable. And to that I say fiddlesticks!'
- 'You'll be living in a world that'll forgotten all these Capital versus Labour agitations.'
- 'Let's say in 1940... There will be peace and prosperity and rapid progress.'

Reveals Birling to be a social climber and is trying to ingratiate himself with the Crofts:

- 'Finchley told me it's exactly the same port your father gets from him.'

Reveals Birling to be a hard-headed businessman who is only interested in profit and not about the community:

- 'a man has to mind his own business and look after his own.'
- 'We employers are coming together to see that our interests, the interests of capital are properly protected.'
- 'If you don't come down sharply on some of these people, they'll soon be asking for the earth.'
- 'Community and all that nonsense.'

Tries to impress and even intimidate the Inspector:

- 'I was alderman for years – and mayor two years ago…I know the Brumley police officers pretty well.'

Critical of Eva Smith and his excuse for firing her:

- 'She had a lot to say – far too much so she had to go.'

Reveals his dislike for socialists and those who wish to improve/change society (referring to the Inspector):

- 'He was prejudiced from the start. Probably a Socialist or some sort of crank – he talked like one.'

Mrs Birling

Stage direction describing her:

- 'rather cold woman and her husband's social superior.'

Reveals she doesn't know her children well:

- 'The things you girls pick up these days.'
- 'you're not that type, you don't get drunk.'

Reveals she understands that men and women are treated and behave differently:

- 'you'll realise that men with important work to do, sometimes have to spend nearly all their time and energy on their business.'

Reveals her prejudice about people (mainly women) from lower classes and how she is unlikely to change:

- 'As if a girl of that sort would ever refuse money.'
- 'I don't suppose for a moment that we can understand why the girl committed suicide. Girls of that class…'
- 'Yes I think it was simply a piece of gross impertinence – quite deliberate – and naturally that was one of the things that prejudiced me against her case.'
- 'He should be made an example of. If the girl's death is due to anybody, then it's due to him.'
- 'I did nothing I'm ashamed of.'

Sheila

Stage direction describing her:

- 'very pretty girl in her early twenties, very pleased with life and rather excited.'

Reveals Sheila to be different to her parents in her attitude to others:

- 'these girls aren't cheap labour – they're people.'

- 'You're beginning to pretend now that nothing's really happened at all.'
- 'If I could help her now, I would.'
- 'I know I'm to blame and I'm desperately sorry.'

Reveals how spoilt she is at the beginning of the play:

- 'because I was in a furious temper.'
- 'But she was very pretty and looked as if she could take care of herself. I couldn't be sorry for her.'

Reveals she's a strong character and is prepared to stand up for herself:

- 'All right Gerald, you needn't look at me like that. At least I'm trying to tell the truth. I expect you've done things you're ashamed of too.'
- 'I tell you – whoever that inspector was, it was anything but a joke.'
- 'I am not a child, don't forget. I've a right to know.'
- 'It frightens me the way you talk, and I can't listen to it anymore.'

Eric

Stage direction describing him:

- 'not quite at ease, half shy, half assertive.'

Reveals that he thinks about others in the community:

- 'Why shouldn't they try for higher wages?'
- 'It's still the same rotten story whether it's been told to a police inspector or to somebody else…It's what happened to the girl and what we all did to her that matters.'

- 'I don't see much nonsense about it when a girl goes and kills herself. You lot may be letting yourselves out nicely, but I can't. Nor can mother. We did her in all right.'
- 'we all helped to kill her.'

Demonstrates that he is not close to his father:

- 'not the kind of father a chap could go to when he's in trouble.'

Gerald

Stage direction describing him:

- 'attractive chap, rather too manly to be a dandy, but very much the easy well-bred, young man-about-town.'

Reveals the way he thinks about working-class women and his own hypocrisy:

- 'I hate those hard eyed, dough-faced women. But then I noticed a girl who looked quite different. She was very pretty.'

Reveals how he didn't care about Daisy's welfare or of what became of her:

- 'I didn't install her there so that I could make love to her...Daisy knew it was coming to an end.'

Glossary

Capitalism – The belief in individual freedom, especially concerning financial matters.

Caricature – a description of a person in which certain characteristics are exaggerated.

Dandy – a man who is very concerned about the way he looks.

Decanter – usually a crystal bottle used for serving port or sherry.

Depression – The Depression was one of the worst banking crises in history and lasted from 1929 to 1939. It resulted in widespread unemployment and poverty.

Edwardian – The Edwardian era was the period of Edward VII's reign from 1901 to 1910.

Etiquette – customs or behaviour used among a particular group or class of people, mostly the upper-classes, for example serving port from a decanter, or wearing formal dress for dinner.

Exploitation – the act of treating someone unfairly in order to benefit from them.

Euphemism – a word or expression used instead of one that is considered too harsh or vulgar. For example, the term 'flower girl' was a euphemism for a prostitute.

Façade – a false or misleading appearance.

General Strike – The General Strike began on 3rd May 1926 and lasted for nine days. It was organised by the Trade Unions (organisations that supported workers) to call for higher wages and complain about working conditions in the factories.

Gluttony – to be very greedy.

Hypocrisy/ Hypocrite – claiming to have higher standards or more noble beliefs than is the case. For example, Mrs Birling is the chairwoman of a charity, but she refuses to support Eva Smith who asked for charity.

Juxtapose – to look at two contrasting ideas side by side.

Lust – strong sexual desire.

Microcosm – a miniature version of something much bigger.

Moral/morality – to have standards of good or correct behaviour.

Oppression – unfair treatment of an individual, social class or population.

Patriarchal – a society, group or situation where men are in control.

Patriotic – to be an enthusiastic (even passionate) supporter of one's country.

Playwright – a person who writes plays.

Portentous – self-important, pleased with himself.

Pride – a feeling of deep pleasure about your achievements.

Prolific – very productive.

Prophet – a religious teacher with an ability to predict the future.

Pseudonym – a fake or different name that a person works under.

Sloth – laziness.

Socialist – a person who believes in a fairer, more equal society.

Sycophantic – behaving in a way to gain someone's favour.

Victorian – The Victorian era was the period of Queen Victoria's reign from 1837 to 1901.

Wall Street – the financial district of New York City.

Wrath – rage, extreme anger.

~ Revision and exam help ~

Exam preparation

Your best preparation for the exam is to get to know the play as well as you can. This does not mean just the plot, but all the analysis, characters, themes, form, structure and language that are covered in this guide. However, in order to do this to the best of your ability, you need to know what the exam is testing you on.

Assessment objectives

Assessment objectives simply means "what you are being tested on". The exam will assess you on four main skills:

Assessment objective	What It says	What It means
AO1	Read, understand and respond to texts. Students should be able to: • maintain a critical style and develop an informed personal response • use textual references, including quotations, to support and illustrate interpretations	• This is checking if you have understood the main elements of the **plot, characters, themes and relationships** in the text. • You need to create **arguments based on your personal opinions** of the characters, themes and relationships. • You need to use **quotations and examples** that prove the arguments you are making.

AO2	Analyse the language, form and structure used by a writer to create meanings and effects, using relevant subject terminology where appropriate	• You need to back up the arguments you are making by analysing **how language, form and structure help to prove your point**. • You need to analyse **the writer's purpose or intention when using these techniques** and what they are trying to make the audience think, learn or feel. • You need to use **the correct terms** when identifying language, form and structure.
AO3	Show understanding of the relationships between texts and the contexts in which they were written	• You need to explain **how the writer was influenced** by the following during the time that the text was written: - What was happening **in society and politics** - What was happening **in literature** - What was happening to **the playwright personally**.

AO4	Use a range of vocabulary and sentence structures for clarity, purpose and effect, with accurate spelling and punctuation	<ul><li>This checks that you are using: wide-ranging and ambitious vocabulary; simple, compound and complex sentences correctly; and that your spelling and punctuation are accurate.</li><li>5% of the marks in English Literature are for spelling, grammar and punctuation, so make sure you proof-read your work to get these marks.</li></ul>

Mapping your revision – The "Journey"

Every character, theme and relationship goes on a journey through the play; this is not a physical journey, but what this means is that they will either change, grow or develop from the beginning to the end of the play. For a clear way to revise, follow these steps:

1. Choose a character, theme or relationship to revise. The sub-headings in this guide are a great place to start. Now find the important pages for your chosen area of revision in this guide. As an example, the character of Sheila Birling is completed below.

2. Write down what you think the writer's overall purpose is for this character/theme/relationship using the information you read in the guide. For example: "Priestley's purpose for Sheila was to

demonstrate the hope he had in the younger generation in changing their thinking for a more socialist future."

3. The first question that you should ask yourself is: "How does the character/theme/relationship change, grow or develop during the text?" Now, plot these on an arrow that represents the beginning to the end. Choose what you think are the top five key moments:

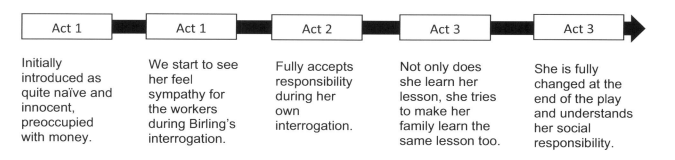

Act 1	Act 1	Act 2	Act 3	Act 3
Initially introduced as quite naïve and innocent, preoccupied with money.	We start to see her feel sympathy for the workers during Birling's interrogation.	Fully accepts responsibility during her own interrogation.	Not only does she learn her lesson, she tries to make her family learn the same lesson too.	She is fully changed at the end of the play and understands her social responsibility.

4. Choose key quotations that are the **best** example of what you have said about the character/theme/relationship. For example:

Act 1

We start to see her feel sympathy for the workers during Birling's interrogation.

"'But these girls aren't cheap labour – they're people"

5. Analyse the language, form or structure of your chosen quotation. You could also choose to discuss the importance of where this scene appears in the text. For example:

"'But these girls aren't cheap labour – they're people"

Sheila personifies the workers in Birling's factory by changing her father's language from "labour" to "people", reflecting her changing attitude towards the working-classes.

6. Add important contextual information that you think has influenced the writer in making the choice that they have made. You may not need this for every key moment you have chosen. There is also no need to repeat yourself! For example:

| Act 1 |

We start to see her feel sympathy for the workers during Birling's interrogation.

The working classes had to work hard for very little money and in terrible working conditions as there was no one to protect their interests. Sheila is beginning to represent the political swing in society towards the welfare of workers.

Once you have done this, you have revised everything that you need to know about the character/theme/relationship, and you have used this revision guide in a really meaningful way. It also means that you should have the information you need to answer an exam question on your chosen area of revision.

Remember: if you know the text well enough, there is nothing you can't answer!

The exam question

The type of question that you will be asked will depend on which exam board your school is entering you for. The most popular exam boards that examine An Inspector Calls are:

Exam Board	What Paper it will be on	What you will be asked to do in the exam
AQA	Paper 2	There is a choice of questions, which do not have extracts. Answer either question on a character/ theme/relationship in the play as a whole. AO4 is marked in this question.
Edexcel	Paper 1	There is a choice of questions, which do not have extracts. Answer either question on a character/ theme/relationship in the play as a whole. AO4 is marked in this question.
Eduquas	Component 2	There is no choice. Answer one question about a particular character/theme/relationship in the extract and the text as a whole. AO4 is marked in this question; AO3 is not.
OCR	Component 1	There is no choice. There are two parts to the question: A and B. Answer Part A as a comparison of an extract from An Inspector Calls with a modern extract from the same genre. Answer Part B on a related character/ theme/relationship from the rest of the play.

Remember: it is important to know which exam board you are studying! Double check with your teacher so that you revise correctly.

Answering the question

1. Read the question twice so that you fully understand what it is asking you to do.

2. Underline the character/theme/relationship that you are being asked to answer on. This will be the focus of your answer. Underline any other key words and phrases that are important. **Hint**: every year the wording of the question will stay the same. The only thing that will change will be the focus of the question; the changing words are what you should be underlining as this will tell you exactly what you need to answer on.

3. If you are asked to answer on an extract, read it through twice. The first time, just read it through so you understand what is happening. The second time, underline important words or phrases that will help you to answer the question.

> How does Priestley present Sheila as a strong character in the play?

Your focus is on Sheila, specifically your opinion about whether or not she is strong.

Important exam question language

Exam questions are worded in a similar way every year. This is why it is important that you know exactly what they mean.

Key word	What it means
Explore/Explain	This means that you should make three or four points about the character, theme or relationship so that you have gone into enough detail.
Attitudes to	You are being asked to discuss the way a character/lots of characters think and feel about a particular theme, which may show in the way they behave towards something.
How Priestley uses	"How" asks you to look at Priestley's techniques, such as the language, form and structure of the text to support the arguments you have made.
How far you agree	You will have been given a statement and you can choose to agree or disagree (or both!) with this statement, using evidence from the text.
Refer to	This means what you should mention specifically in your answer.

Planning your answer

This is one of the most important parts of what you will do in the exam! The majority of the marks you get are based on whether you develop your argument and you cannot do that if you haven't planned. It will also help you feel calm and less overwhelmed in the exam. Planning also helps you to choose the best ideas that match your argument, rather than the first one that comes to your head.

The step-by-step approach to the five-minute plan

1. Brainstorm or bullet point everything you remember about the character, theme or relationship you have been asked about. Empty your head! This should take no longer than thirty seconds. Make sure you include at least one idea from the extract if you have been given one.

2. Write down the numbers 1-5 on your planning sheet, leaving space to jot your ideas down. This will be the basic structure of your answer. This is what you should write beside each number:

   1: Write a summary of the journey that the character, theme or relationship takes during the play. Just write one to two sentences.

   2-4: Use your brainstorming from Step 1 to choose the three key moments in the text that demonstrate the argument you have created. You will have loads in your brainstorm, but you must now choose **the best ideas**. Remember, if there is an extract, make sure to include at least one idea from the extract.

   5: Sum up your main point and write down what you think the playwright's purpose was for creating the character, theme or relationship like this.

3. Go back over your plan and include the best quotes for **2-4**. You do not need any additional quotes in your introduction or conclusion.

4. Read over your plan. Add any context or language techniques that you remember from your revision. This way, when you use your plan to write your answer, you won't forget to add this important information. You might also want to juggle around the paragraphs if you think they would work better in another order.

> Key moment from Act 1 (Step 2)

> Language analysis is included using the correct term (Step 4)

Example plan for how Sheila is presented in An Inspector Calls

1. Sheila – goes through a significant change from the beginning to the end of the play, from a selfish, naïve girl who lacked knowledge about the society she lived in, to a more socially aware citizen who understands her social responsibility.

2. Beginning: Initially introduced as quite naïve and innocent, preoccupied with money: '(Excited) Oh – Gerald – you've got it – is it the one [ring] you wanted me to have?' The ring is a symbol of a love based on money and financial gain, rather a romantic form of love.

3. Changes when she is interrogated by the Inspector and immediately regrets her actions in Milwards: 'I know I'm to blame – and I'm desperately sorry'.

4. She learns her lesson. She takes responsibility and changes from a girl preoccupied with her own life to a more socially aware, responsible citizen; she also tries to encourage the members of her family to do the same: 'I remember what he said, how he looked and what he made me feel. Fire and blood and anguish'.

5. Priestley's purpose for Sheila was that she gives the audience hope that their society can improve if people make changes and take responsibility.

> Best quote to show her change (Step 3)

Golden rules of planning

1. Only give yourself five minutes at the beginning of each question. The plan itself doesn't get any marks so any longer will just eat into your essay-writing time.

2. Look back at your plan before you write a paragraph. This will keep you on track and will make sure you don't forget anything you want to say.

3. Use a full page to plan out your response. You don't have to worry about running out of space in your exam booklet; you can always ask for more paper.

Writing introductions

Your introduction is the first impression you will make on an examiner, so it is important that it has an impact to get you the grade you deserve.

Your introduction is Step 1 from your plan, which you will now develop:

1: Write a summary of the journey that the character, theme or relationship takes during the text.

- Make sure that you answer the question in detail, talking about how the character, theme or relationship changes, grows or develops from the beginning to the end.
- Make sure that the points of the question that you talk about are what is on your plan – your examiner will then have a really clear idea what you are going to talk about.
- Explain the playwright's purpose for this character, theme or relationship. What message are they trying to get across to their audiences by including this?
- You could start by using words from the question in your introduction to help you begin.

Example Introduction: Explore how the character of Sheila is presented in An Inspector Calls

In the play An Inspector Calls, Priestley presents Sheila as a character that undergoes a transformation throughout the play. She changes from being a young, innocent girl, who was very ignorant of society's problems, to a more socially aware and responsible citizen who becomes very disillusioned with her family's beliefs. Through Sheila, Priestley suggests that reforms to society must be made in order for society to progress at all and by using Sheila, he is suggesting that it is the younger generation who can make these changes.

Writing main paragraphs

This is the section where you are going to get the bulk of your marks. This is the opportunity for you to expand on what you have said in your introduction and really develop your arguments.

Your main paragraphs are Steps 2-4 of your plan, which you will now develop:

> **2-4:** Use your brainstorming from Step 1 to choose the three key moments in the text that demonstrate the argument you have created. You will have loads in your brainstorm, but you must now choose **the best ideas**. Remember, if there is an extract, make sure to include at least one idea from the extract.

Paragraph structure

AO1: Answer the question. How/why does the character/theme change from previously?
AO3: Links made to context
AO1: Short, embedded quote and explanation of how the quote proves the point
AO2: Analysis of language or structure to support argument
AO2: Writer's purpose – why has Priestley included this scene/character and what is the effect?

The paragraph structure to the left will help you to develop your argument fully to make sure that you meet all of the assessment objectives.

AO1: Your argument and opinions and your ability to back up your arguments with evidence from the text.

AO2: Your analysis of language and structure, as well as your explanation of why the writer makes the decisions they did.

AO3: Your explanation of how the text links to the context. This is done best when it is linked to your argument.

Example main paragraph: Explore how the character of Sheila is presented in An Inspector Calls (argument from Act 1)

AO1: argument	Within Act 1 of the play, after the Inspector has arrived, it is clear to see Priestley exposes the audience to a changing Sheila, when she begins to show sympathy
AO3: context linked	for the working class girls in Birling's factory. She is shocked by the way that her father speaks about the girls and expresses this shock very clearly. With this statement, it is as if Sheila is echoing the Suffragette movement, who fought for equal rights of women and battled to ensure that they were treated as fairly as other members of society. Responding to a point Mr Birling previously makes, Sheila retorts by saying
AO1: quotation	"these girls aren't cheap labour, they're people", which
AO2: language analysis	demonstrates how she recognises her father's poor treatment of the working girls in his factory, like Eva Smith. Sheila personifies the workers in Birling's factory by changing her father's language from "labour" to "people", reflecting her changing attitude towards the working classes. She clearly empathises with them by
AO2: Writer's Purpose	juxtaposing a commodity like "labour" with a living thing like "people". The audience begin to realise that Sheila is a device used by Priestley to drive his socialist ideas forward, whilst simultaneously projecting the idea that she is a woman before her time.

Dos and don'ts when writing main paragraphs

Do

- Link your paragraphs together to create a "flow" in your essay. Refer back to what you said previously.

- Write more than one sentence for each part of the paragraph structure. Explain yourself fully!

- Give more than one interpretation of language/structure if you can and only if it links to the argument you are making.

- Make sure that every part of the structure refers back to the first sentence and your overall argument.

Don't

- Repeat context that you have said before. It is not necessary to put context in every paragraph if it means you are just repeating yourself.

- Use the same sentence starters for all three paragraphs. Your writing will sound like you are filling in the blanks!

- Forget to always say "why". Why has the character changed? Why has the writer used that language technique? Why does that quote prove your point?

Writing conclusions

If your introduction is your first impression, then the conclusion is the last impression that you leave with the examiner before they award you a mark. That's why it needs to be punchy, impactful and meaningful!

Your conclusion is Step 5 from your plan, which you will now develop:

> **5:** Sum up your main point and write down what you think the playwright's purpose was for creating the character, theme or relationship like this.

- Make sure that you summarise the journey that the character or theme has been on in one to two sentences.

- Explain the writer's overall purpose for this character, theme or relationship. What is their big message that they are trying to get across?

- Don't introduce any new ideas – this is your opportunity to summarise your key arguments.

Example Conclusion: Explore how the character of Sheila is presented in An Inspector Calls

In conclusion, Priestley reveals a fully changed character to his audience by the end of the play. Sheila has undergone such a dramatic change that the audience no longer recognise her from the innocent, preoccupied girl that they met in Act 1. Instead, the audience are left with an enlightened woman, who understands the role she must play in modern society. Priestley's purpose for Sheila was that she gives the audience hope that their society can improve if people make changes and take responsibility.

Using quotations in the exam

The whole point of having quotations in your response is to prove the arguments that you make. However, that doesn't mean you have to learn the whole play off by heart!

Tips and tricks for using quotations

1. Look at the key quotations on page 54 of this revision guide.
2. Choose the quotations that **best** prove the point you are trying to make about the character, theme or relationship.
3. Keep your quotations to a couple of words or a phrase. Don't write long amounts of text in your answer. Just stick to the part that actually proves what you are saying.
4. Try to embed your quotations into the sentence rather than saying: "this can be seen in the quote". This simply means making the quotations part of your own sentence.
5. Always use quotation marks!

Not embedded:

Sheila is initially introduced by Priestley as quite a naïve and innocent girl, who is preoccupied with money. This can be seen in the quote: '(Excited) Oh – Gerald – you've got it – is it the one [ring] you wanted me to have?'

Embedded:

Sheila is initially introduced by Priestley as quite naïve and innocent girl, who is preoccupied with money. When she is given her engagement ring by Gerald, she responds in an 'excited' way by asking him whether it is 'the one you wanted me to have?'

Here is another example:

Not embedded:

Sheila changes when she is interrogated by the Inspector and immediately regrets her actions in Milwards. This can be seen in the quote: 'I know I'm to blame – and I'm desperately sorry'.

Embedded:

Sheila changes when she is interrogated by the Inspector and immediately regrets her actions in Milwards. She says that she 'know(s) I'm to blame' and describes herself as 'desperately sorry' for her actions.

It may seem like only a small change to embed the quotation, but it will help the examiner to follow what you are saying more easily and will make your paragraph "flow".

Improving your written expression

AO1, the first assessment objective, talks about the "style" of your writing. It must be formal and critical, meaning that it should feel balanced and not too over-the-top.

Sentence starters to avoid and sophisticated substitutions

When you use the same sentence starters and phrases in an essay, it can feel stiff and unnatural to read. These are some simple changes you can make so that your essay sounds more formal and will help you to vary your response:

Avoid overusing...	Use instead...
"Priestley **presents** Sheila as..."	• Priestley **illustrates** Sheila as... • Priestley **portrays** Sheila as... • Priestley **depicts** Sheila as... • Priestley **reveals** Sheila as...to the audience • Priestley **paints** Sheila as...
"This **shows**..."	• This **suggests**... • This **indicates**... • This **implies** ... • This **infers**...
"I think/I feel/I believe..." **(never use "I" in an essay)**	• It could be argued that... • The audience is left with the impression that... • The audience is positioned to feel that... • This could be interpreted as...
"The character **represents**..."	• The character **symbolises**... • The character **embodies**... • The character **reflects**... • The character **epitomises**... • The character **typifies**... • The character **exemplifies**...

Joining ideas and paragraphs together

If you start every single paragraph with the same word or in the same way, then it will get boring for the examiner.

1. Use adding and contrasting connectives to make connections between your paragraphs and improve the fluency of your writing.
   Adding connectives: 'In addition', 'Moreover', 'Furthermore', 'Similarly', 'As well as', 'Consequently'.
   Contrasting connectives: 'In contrast', 'However', 'Alternatively', 'On the other hand', 'Whereas'.

2. Add signposts for the examiner at the beginning of your paragraphs to let them know the part of the text you will be talking about.
   Signposts: 'At the beginning of the play', 'Later on, in Act 3', 'Finally', 'Eventually', 'In conclusion'.

Using evaluative adjectives

Adjective	Example
Skilful/Skilfully	Priestley **skilfully** uses the character of Sheila to…
Subtle/Subtly	The use of … is a **subtle** hint that…
Pivotal	This **pivotal** moment in the play means the audience is positioned to feel…
Effective	This is an **effective** method employed by Priestley to…
Striking	This **striking** image serves to…
Challenging	This is a **challenging** moment in the play that allows the audience to…
Central concern	The theme of … is a **central concern** to the play.
Significant	This is particularly **significant** because…

Just like in English Language, you may wish to make a judgement about how successful the playwright has been in achieving their purpose. This is another way of achieving the "critical style" that AO1 sets out. You could do this by using the following adjectives:

Some further sophisticated analytical tips

1. Analysing an alternative interpretation:

   - The phrase could also be interpreted as revealing…

2. Analysing the combined effect of several techniques together:

   - The writer uses _____ coupled with_____ to illustrate…

3. Tracking how key ideas are developed through a text

   - This idea is further developed when…

4. Deepening the analysis of a character/theme:

   - On the exterior _____, yet on further inspection of the character the audience sees…

   - At first glance _____; however, on closer inspection the audience learns…

Making the main paragraph even more analytical

Let's look back at the example main paragraph from earlier and see all of these written expressions in action:

Signpost

Evaluative adjective

Evaluative adjective

Within Act 1 of the play, after the Inspector has arrived, Priestley **skilfully** exposes the audience to a changing Sheila, when she begins to show sympathy for the working class girls in Birling's factory. She is shocked by the way that her father speaks about the girls and expresses this shock very clearly. With this statement, it is as if Sheila is echoing the Suffragette movement, who fought for equal rights of women and battled to ensure that they were treated as fairly as other members of society. Responding to a point Mr Birling previously makes, Sheila retorts by saying "these girls aren't cheap labour, they're people", which demonstrates **effectively** how she recognises her father's poor treatment of the working girls in his factory, like Eva Smith. Sheila personifies the workers in Birling's factory by changing her father's language from "labour" to "people", reflecting her changing attitude towards the working classes. **At first glance, it seems like she is just giving her opinion, but on deeper inspection, she is also criticising her father.** She clearly empathises with them by juxtaposing a commodity like "labour" with a living thing like "people". **The audience is left with the impression** that Sheila **is a device** used by Priestley to drive his socialist ideas forward, whilst simultaneously projecting the idea that she is a woman before her time, **which is a central concern to the play.**

Deepening analysis

Sophisticated substitution

Evaluative adjective

~ Progress and revision check answers ~

Background information

1. The town has a Lord Mayor; there is a charity to help young women in need; and the town has a Chief Constable of police.

2. Socialism is based on giving the workers (the people who make and manufacture goods) the profit from their work directly, whereas capitalism is an economic and political system in which a country's trade and industry are controlled by private owners who make a profit.

3. Arthur Birling and The Crofts.

4. The Inspector.

5. Mrs Birling and Sir George and Lady Croft.

6. Eva Smith.

7. Soldiers returned home in 1918 to unemployment, strikes and protests.

8. It is an example of a post-war drama, exploring the economic, social and political issues at the end of the Second World War, but it also focuses on life for all classes before the First World War.

9. The play is a challenge to the audience to think about how many more disasters might lie ahead if we don't learn from past mistakes.

10. The Welfare state which included The National Health Service (NHS) and the introduction of free education.

The play – summary and analysis

1. They suggest that although the family is materially well-off and wealthy, they are not really happy on the inside.

2. They are celebrating Sheila and Gerald Croft's engagement.

3. Sheila is described as 'pretty' and 'lively' whilst Eric is presented as being 'awkward' and almost drunk.

4. Post-war audiences would have appreciated the dramatic irony, knowing that Arthur Birling was wrong about everything.

5. Birling is only interested in making a profit for himself. In firing workers for asking for higher wages, he demonstrates a lack of concern for their welfare.

6. He is hypocritical because on the one hand he wants to protect Sheila but on the other he was quite happy to abandon Daisy Renton.

7. The younger Birlings are more impressionable than their parents or Gerald which makes them more open to the Inspector's message about social responsibility.

8. The Inspector's use of the photograph of the girl and the 'rough sort of diary' are convenient devices to explain his close knowledge of events.

9. It is convenient because it is used to question the very existence of Eva Smith.

10. It is significant because it's the only place in town where men of Gerald and Eric's class would meet working-class women and prostitutes and it represents the higher class men's abuse of their position.

Characters

1. He acts as the storyteller linking the separate incidents into one storyline and often supplies dates or fills in the background. He behaves like a priest to each character, encouraging them to confess their guilt for what happened to Eva Smith.

2. Like his home, Birling is also heavy, 'portentous' and 'substantial.' He also lacks affection for his children. There is nothing 'cosy' about him.

3. He doesn't know his children well and he is not the kind of father a son would go to when in trouble.

4. She is the chairwoman of a charity that is supposed to help women in need and yet she rejects Eva's request for help.

5. She is presented as being rather innocent, childish but lively.

6. At the beginning of the play she responds to her father with, 'But these girls aren't cheap labour – they're people.' Later she retorts with, 'I tell you - whoever that inspector was, it was anything but a joke.'

7. The stage directions describe him as, 'not quite at ease, half shy, half assertive.' His immaturity and his lack of awareness of social etiquette is shown when he 'suddenly guffaws,' a clear indication that he feels uncomfortable in social situations and is unsure of how to behave.

8. He has a very formal relationship with his father whom he does not find easy to approach.

9. Being about thirty, he is older than Sheila and Eric whose parents treat Gerald as an equal. Moreover, he is already a businessman and agrees with Birling on how business should be conducted.

10. She is kind, caring and hard-working and unlike the Birlings, ends up being poor and homeless.

Themes

1. The Inspector could be Priestley's mouthpiece because he uses his final speech to reinforce the key ideas of social responsibility that Priestley was so keen to get across.

2. Birling ignores the needs of his workers, Mrs Birling as chairwoman of a local charity fails to help those who really need it, Gerald abandons Eva, Sheila as an influential customer shouldn't have abused her power and Eric drinks too much causing him to abuse Eva.

3. Both Sheila and Eric learn this lesson. They learn that it's important to look after other people in society and not to behave selfishly.

4. After the Inspector has left the house, Mr and Mrs Birling think things can go back to how they were before he came. Mrs Birling claims she was innocent of all dealings with Eva Smith and blames Eric. This is perhaps one reason why the play ends with a call from the police station informing them that an inspector is on his way. They have not learned any lessons.

5. Birling married Sybil to secure his status as a middle-class businessman.

6. Birling brought wealth to the marriage.

7. Men were expected to be 'busy with work,' whilst women were expected to be interested in less important matters such as shopping and weddings.

8. Both men abuse her body for their own sexual pleasure.

9. They are referred to as 'boy' and 'girl;' both are ordered around by their parents even though they are young adults.

10. She is defined by her role as a servant and not as a person in the same way as Eva is defined as a 'worker.'

Form, structure and language

1. The drama takes place in one setting in real time; the characters' manner of speech is realistic; the setting is realistic and so are the local references to the town.

2. He changes the mood and atmosphere by changing the lighting in different scenes.

3. The play tries to teach the audience lessons that focused on the seven deadly sins: lust, gluttony, greed, sloth, wrath, envy and pride. The Inspector also sets out to teach the Birlings and Gerald a lesson in social responsibility.

4. It is like a crime thriller because the audience receive clues about who has committed the crime and will enjoy trying to guess what happened before the end of the action.

5. Euphemisms are an attempt to disguise the seriousness of something.

6. Mrs Birling's language is more formal and grammatically correct than the language used by the other characters, suggesting a higher degree of education. Unlike the others, she rarely asks questions which suggests that she is self-confident.

7. Alcohol and the drinking of alcohol could symbolise corruption and improper social behaviour. Alderman Meggarty was drunk when he confronts Eva Smith in the Palace Bar; Eric is drunk when he forces himself on Eva Smith; and Birling offers the Inspector a drink in order to soften him up, something that would be considered very inappropriate.

8. The Inspector asks many more questions than the other characters as a policeman would be expected to. He speaks bluntly and clearly and to the point. The one exception to this is his final speech in which he sounds more like a preacher.

9. Sheila uses the image of a wall to describe her mother's attempt to avoid responsibility and her refusal to accept the reality of what has happened.

10. Birling has Eva removed from his factory and then Sheila has her fired from the shop. Gerald allows Eva access to a hotel and his friend's flat, but then removes her from it. Eric takes away Eva's right to her own personal space by forcing himself upon her.

Printed in Great Britain
by Amazon